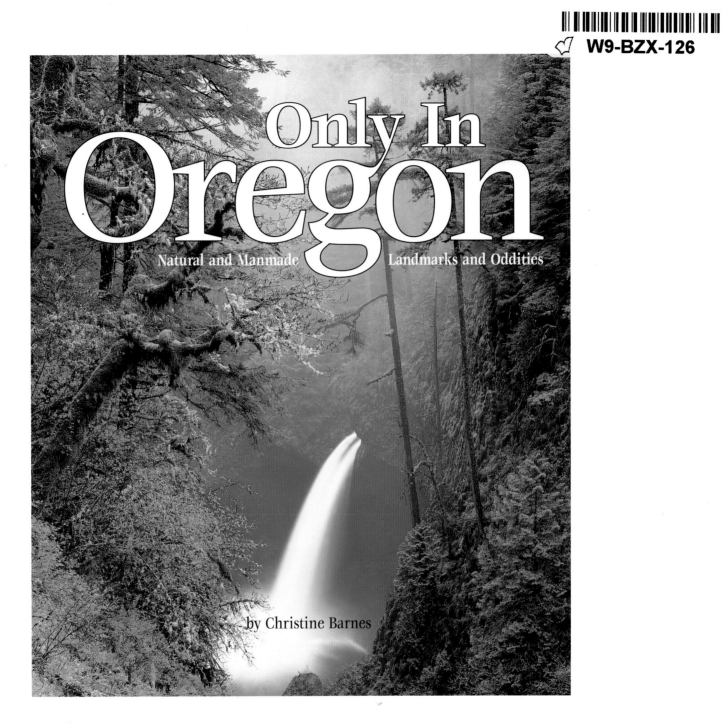

Only In
Oregon

Natural and Manmade   Landmarks and Oddities

by Christine Barnes

FARCOUNTRY
PRESS

For Jackson, Maya & Elliott
a little fodder for your curious minds

I wish to thank the Oregon Department of Transportation staff whose tips on roadside sites led us through the state: Dwayne Barber, Jeanette Kloos, Dan Knoll, Mary Lauzon, Julie Schablitsky, Michael Schaff, Tom Strandberg and Laura Trott. Also, the Bureau of Land Management, The Columbia River Inter-Tribal Fish Commission, Oregon Department of Fish and Wildlife, Oregon Emergency Management, Oregon Forestry Department, Oregon State Parks, Oregon Travel Information Council, Portland, Oregon Visitors Association, Portland Parks and Recreation, 1000 Friends of Oregon and dozens of chambers of commerce, visitors center and historical societies staff and volunteers who all offered information.

A special thanks to my photographer, husband and driver, Jerry Barnes, whose enthusiasm made every wrong turn an adventure, and whose images captured what I could not say in words.

ISBN 1-56037-292-3
Text © 2004 by Christine Barnes
© 2004 Farcountry Press

For more information about our books write Farcountry Press, P.O. Box 5630, Helena, MT 59604; call (800) 821-3874; or visit www.farcountrypress.com.

Created, produced, and designed in the United States.
Printed in Korea.

08 07 06 05 04   1 2 3 4 5

Table of Contents

Oregon

Sunrise near Corvallis

There are landmarks and then there are LANDMARKS—
places that make this 96,000-square-mile patch of
America so special to so many. Since statehood on
February 14, 1859, Oregonians have been searching,
discovering, creating, and sometimes destroying
these treasures.

The challenge for this book was to select fewer than
one hundred of those Only in Oregon destinations—
including a few of the best known, such as Crater
Lake, and the more obscure—and tell each story.

With the state divided into six regions thanks to the
Oregon Tourism Commission guidelines (with a little
fudging of boundaries), I packed up the car and my
husband and his camera, then set out to really *see*
Oregon one region at a time. After a decade of calling
the state our home, it became clear: we were in for a
learning experience.

The places selected are as significant as a stop along
the Oregon Trail, where pioneers overcame incredible
odds to homestead the Pacific Northwest, or as quirky
as the lava rock Dee Wright Observatory perched along
the McKenzie Highway in one of the country's largest
lava fields. And then we have that huge Hole-in-the-
Ground near Christmas Valley in eastern Oregon—not
to be confused with Big Hole seven miles away. And
you probably know that the Cascade Range is volcanic,
but how did that funny looking point form on top of
Mt. Washington?

We know manmade things are bound to be odd:
consider the source. But who would have put an
underground whale that spouts water over a lawn
every minute-on-the-minute in a postage stamp-size
park in the coastal town of Yachats? And what's with
the guy called the "little fellow" who stands atop the
rather unusual state capitol rotunda in Salem? Or
those two towering green glass spires growing from
the Oregon Convention Center in Portland.

Oregon's cultural history has resulted in some interesting spots, like the only Basque handball court in the
state, constructed in 1915. Traditional ways ebb and
flow, but members of the Warm Springs Tribe continue

to dip-net fish for salmon from wooden scaffolds and platforms along the Deschutes River at Sherar's Falls in the same way their ancestors fished for generations.

Then there's the combo of natural and manmade sights/sites. If you've driven along the Pacific Coast Highway, you've surely noticed all of those "myrtlewood" factories selling clocks, bowls, coffee tables, and other handicrafts.... Well, take a detour to Myrtle Point to see a premiere myrtlewood tree standing at the end of the high school football field. More stunning is Simpson Reef, where sea lions and seals haul themselves off Cape Arago, and not far up the coast the exquisite Shore Acres gardens showcasing what man can create.

And just because we love the yin and yang of life, one of the state's great rock formations, Smith Rock in central Oregon, stands only a few miles from Petersen's Rock Garden. One represents a geologic wonder; the other just makes you wonder.

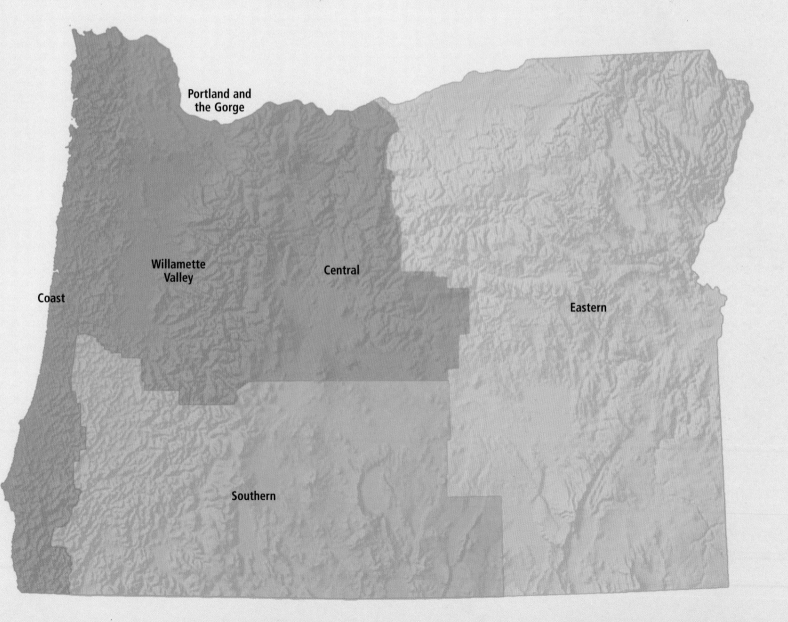

Oregon Coast

The Pacific coastline is the sea's gift to Oregon. Not your placid white sand sun-bathing kind of beach, the Oregon coast is like a 300-mile complex personality that shifts from angry to seductive in an instant, but always with a constant "come hither" attitude with each crashing wave. The shore with sandstone cliffs and rock formations offers a stage for a continuous and evolving chorus line of seals, otters, sea lions, seabirds, and sea creatures. Harbors are still full of fishing boats, and men and women continue to "go to sea," where they risk their lives to make a living.

1. Graveyard of the Pacific
2. Largest Tree
3. Oswald West State Park
4. Tillamook Air Museum
5. Fishermen's Memorial Walk
6. Oregon Coast Aquarium
7. Whale of a Park
8. Myrtlewood Factory
9. *New Carissa*
10. Cape Arago and Shore Acres State Park
11. Coquille Myrtle Grove State Natural Site
12. Faber Farms
13. Prehistoric Gardens

The Needles Seastacks, Cannon Beach

THE ASTORIA COLUMN, A 125-FOOT Romanesque column, tops Coxcomb Hill in Astoria. As landmarks go, it ranks as one of Oregon's most recognizable. But climb the 164 steps to the observatory, and you can see the living history of the region and a nearly invisible landmark that surges with the tides. At the confluence of the Pacific Ocean and the Columbia River, where tons of sand shifts beneath the surface, lurks the Columbia River bar. The dangerous waters between buoys 6 and 10 have earned it the name "Graveyard of the Pacific." And for good reason.

Since Capt. Robert Gray sailed into the mouth of the Columbia River in 1792, 2,000 vessels and 700 people have been lost here. The combination of brutal, churning ocean swells, the flow of the nation's second largest river, and shallow, shifting sandbars warranted an official designation. In 1977 the National Transportation Safety Board declared the Columbia River bar "a specially haz-ardous area," the only such river designation in the 88,533 miles of U.S. coastline. Yet, as treacherous as the Columbia River bar is, more than 300 large ships and tankers carrying passengers, grain, bulk cargo, logs, and oil safely enter the river each month.

Each large vessel is transported through the treacherous mouth of the Columbia by a Columbia River bar pilot. Two pilot boats moored at Hammond Boat Basin, along with a helicopter, stand ready to take a pilot to board a vessel. The pilot determines whether it is safe to make the trip, then takes the helm and maneuvers the vessel in or out of port. The pilot boats then transport the pilot to another ship or bring him back to shore in much the same way as has been done since 1846.

The best place to get a sense of the seafaring history of the area is at the Columbia River Maritime Museum, the kind of interpretive center that can give you chills. Not only is every shipwreck mapped out, but visitors can get up close and personal with a Coast Guard rescue, stand in the cockpit of a tugboat, or view some of the hundreds of displays while listening to old fishermen's tales. You have to believe that most of them are true. Docked beside the museum and open to visitors is the lightship *Columbia,* the last seagoing lighthouse ship to serve on the West Coast. Big ships are best viewed from the cov-ered deck at the end of 6th Street and from the dock at 17th Street, where two Coast Guard cutters, the *Steadfast* and the *Alert,* are stationed and river tour boats come to call.

Up the hill from the museum, recently spruced up in a $5 million renovation, is the town of Astoria. This historic burg, the oldest settlement west of the Rockies, retains the rough-and-tumble charm of a working seaport and fishing town where espressos cost 50 cents and people still "go to sea."

Details: Astoria can be reached from either U.S. 30, which runs along the Columbia River, or U.S. 101. A trolley goes along the waterfront that includes the Columbia River Maritime Museum, 1792 Marine Dr., (503) 325-2323, www.crmm.org.

Other Astoria Assets

Lewis and Clark: Tourists have been flooding into Astoria as they follow the Lewis and Clark Trail and tour the 1950s replica of Fort Clatsop, the 1805/06 winter resting spot for the Corps of Discovery. There are about twenty other Lewis and Clark sites in the area.

Flavel House: The restored Queen Anne–style home of Astoria's wealthiest resident, Capt. George Flavel, was saved from the wrecking ball in 1951 by the local historical society. The hills around Astoria are filled with less spectacular, but still interesting, Victorian homes. Some like to call Astoria the little San Francisco of the Northwest—"little" at a population of 10,000.

Union Town: Historic Union Town at the foot of the Astoria-Megler Bridge (at 4 miles, the longest bridge in Oregon) features Suomi Hall, established by the Finnish Brotherhood in 1886, a Finnish meat market, and "authentic" Finnish steambath that seems to have taken on more modern tenants such as adult "entertainment."

Fort Stevens State Park: Originally commissioned as a Civil War fortification in 1863, Fort Stevens was deactivated as a military fort shortly after World War II. It is now an Oregon state park with miles of beach and a historical military site and museum.

Peter Iredale: On Nov. 10, 1906, the four-masted British sailing vessel *Peter Iredale* wrecked at Clatsop Beach. A crew of twenty-seven and two stowaways were rescued by the U.S. life-saving crew at Hammond. Remains of the *Peter Iredale* are embedded on the beach of Fort Stevens State Park.

Kindergarten Cop: Yes, Arnold (the actor and governor of California) Schwarzenegger's movie was filmed at Astor school. *Free Willy I* and *II* and Stephen Spielberg's *Goonies* are a few of the other movies with Astoria and its waters as a backdrop.

AS FAR AS GOVERNOR'S GO, REPUBLICAN Tom McCall ranks as one of the most flamboyant, savvy, and visionary politicians the state has ever known. During his 1967–1975 governorship, his vision and drive shaped Oregon. It still does.

As McCall biographer Brent Walth puts it in *Fire at Eden's Gate,* "More than other American political leaders of his time, Tom McCall personified the sweeping environmental movement of the 1960s and 1970s. While other politicians had talked of the need to clean and protect the nation's land, air and water, McCall had acted." One of greatest of these acts occurred on the Oregon coast on May 13, 1967, the day Governor McCall literally drew a line in the sand. The state's beaches had been protected since 1913, when Gov. Oswald West came up with a plan to protect all 312 miles of coastline. Governor West's idea was to draft a bill declaring the seashore from the Washington state line to the California border a public highway, putting the Oregon coastline into public ownership and making its protection feasible. For decades Oregonians assumed the beach was their beach. But the definition of beachfront as only the wet portion of the beach (that at low tide) opened up beachfront development that could block public access.

By 1967, 112 miles of dry sands along the Pacific had been taken over by private owners. The crowning insult came in 1966, when Cannon Beach Surfsand Motel owner William

Hay put up a barricade of logs around a dry sand area adjacent to the motel and posted signs: "Surfsand Guests Only Please." While the state legislature wrangled over a new beach bill, Governor McCall, a former reporter and television anchorman, took the issue to the press—not with your ordinary press conference, but with an entourage of scientists, surveyors, aides, and reporters by helicopters near Seaside. There the governor announced: "The politicians and the lawyers have got this beach situation all fouled up. Now the scientists are here to straighten it out." With that, surveyors began marking new lines that included 16 feet of dry sand, and McCall made his stand.

A towering figure at six-foot-six, the governor glared at the startled sunbathing guests. Then surveyors pounded the first stake near the "private" Surfsand Motel beach with the famous Haystack Rock in the background. McCall and his group flew to four more spots on coast between Seaside and Neskowin, repeating the survey and photo ops.

The House passed a new beach bill that extended the reach of public beaches, giving the state the ability to zone, though not own, the dry sands up to the 16-foot marker.

Details: There are no interpretive markers at these historic and politically charged spots, but walk the Oregon beaches and be thankful for Tom McCall's line in the sand. The Surfsand Motel was sold to Jan and Steve Martin in 1979. Since then, the motel has been operated by the Martin family, remodeled, and expanded into the family-oriented Surfsand Resort.

Oswald West State Park

Originally called Short Sands State Park, the 2,500-acre swath of land includes 13 miles of coastal headlands, Cape Falcon, and Neahkahnie Mt. In the late 1970s it was renamed Oswald West State Park. The park is 10 miles south of Cannon Beach on U.S. 101.

OREGONIANS ARE SERIOUS ABOUT their trees, whether it's saving them or logging them. So, it is an interesting contrast to marvel at the largest living tree in Oregon, in Klootchy Creek County Park, and then to drive by acres of harvested forests.

The 750-year-old Sitka spruce is not only Oregon's largest tree but also the largest specimen of this species in the United States. At 206 feet in height and 56 feet around, it looks like a towering mossy beast. With a base like elephant feet, covered with moss and decorated with a few mushrooms and ferns, it makes you just want to go up and, well, hug it. Wooden railings keep visitors from embracing the tree, with its knobby warts and all. What makes seeing this impressive tree so amazing is that you may have traveled through miles of clear-cut and tree plantations before pulling into Klootchy Park to visit this particular Sitka. At least every second person gazing at the tree asks,

"How did the loggers miss this one?"

The story came to light only in 2000, when the tree was about to be honored with its official dedication as the Oregon Largest Tree and the first tree in Oregon's Heritage Tree program. Retired Salem barber Maynard Dawson worked for 50 years as the Klootchy giant's

biggest advocate and is the man responsible for its designation as Oregon's largest tree. But even he was unsure how it survived the extensive logging of the area's old-growth forests.

Clarence Richen, who read about the upcoming dedication, came forward with the story. As the man responsible for selecting trees to be harvested by Crown Zellerbach during the 1940s, he explained that the giant was "too limby," lacking the quality demanded by the U.S. War Production Board for the construction of aircraft. Once it was passed over, loggers became rather fond of the spruce, pruned out dead limbs, and sprayed it two successive years to save its life. At age 88, Mr. Richen was invited to the dedication, but he died on December 6, 2000, less than a week before the ceremony.

> **Details:** Klootchy Creek County Park is 2.5 miles east of U.S. 101 off U.S. 26 near Seaside.

Tree Factoids

Octopus Tree: If loggers thought the Klootchy giant Sitka was "too limby," one wonders what went through the minds of folks when they got a load of the candelabra-shaped Sitka at Cape Meares, sculpted by the elements of the Oregon coast in one of the state's remaining old-growth forests. The Cape is a National Wildlife Refuge, and huge Sitkas and western hemlocks provide habitat for threatened bird species including bald eagles, marbled murrelets, and northern spotted owls.

What Is a Heritage Tree? The giant Sitka spruce was named the first Heritage Tree in Oregon's Heritage Tree program, the first state-sponsored heritage tree program in the country. It began in 1995 under the auspices of the Travel Information Council and dedicated individuals. Trees designated as Heritage Trees all meet criteria similar to those for National Historic Places: they must be associated with important historic events or people, be significant or distinguishable entities within a community or location, or be of notable age, size, or species. At press time, there were twenty-eight official Oregon Heritage Trees.

Douglas Firs and Christmas Trees: The Klootchy Sitka may be the largest tree in Oregon, but the official state tree, the Douglas fir, is thought to be the tallest. First described by botanist David Douglas in the 1820s (hence its name), Douglas fir trees reach their maximum height in almost pure stands along the Coast Range, with the tallest tree, at 329 feet, on BLM land in Coos County. Folks outside of Oregon probably know the Douglas fir as the most popular Christmas tree in the United States, with noble firs close behind. Oregon produced approximately 8 million Christmas trees in 2003, making it the leading supplier of Christmas conifers in the nation. But it's not just its holiday adaptation that makes the Doug fir Oregon's state tree; it is the state's most economically important tree, used for lumber, plywood, pulp, and holiday décor.

Tree Factoids

Monterey Cypress: Next to the oldest standing house in the Chetco Valley (now the Chetco Valley Museum) stands Oregon's largest Monterey cypress. There's been some discussion on the status of this tree, since another sign notes that it is the largest Monterey cypress in the world. Whatever…it's big.

Clear-cutting: The dictionary definition of clear-cutting is the removal of all trees in a stand of timber. During the past century, clear-cutting has been the primary method of timber harvest in the Pacific Northwest, leaving a patchwork of barren and replanted land amidst dense forests with thousands of miles of logging roads. The definition is a bit different in the Beaver State: according to the Oregon Forest Practices, a minimum of two green trees per acre and one "downed" or standing snag must be left on each clear-cut acre.

Oregon's forests cover about 46 percent of the state's total landmass (approximately 29 million acres), according to the World Forestry Center in Portland. The federal government owns 57 percent of the forested land, much of that in thirteen national forests; 22 percent is held by private industry; 16 percent is with non-industrial private owners; and 3 percent belongs to the state, with the remaining 2 percent in other public ownership.

The state's harvest peaked in 1986 at 8.7 billion board feet, with 56 percent of the logs coming from federal lands. At the low in 2001, the federal land share had dropped to 5 percent, mainly because of environmental pressure on governmental agencies to halt or reduce logging in old growth forests. With the decline of harvesting on federal land, the 100,000 acres clear-cut each year are primarily on private land. The current Oregon Forestry Plan states that a clear-cut can't be larger than 120 acres in a single ownership, and landowners have one year to begin replanting the cleared acreage and two years to complete it.

Douglas fir forests are generally targeted for clear-cutting, since the trees are shade intolerant and newly planted trees can't grow under the canopy of a mature forest or compete with shrubbery and other trees. In addition to providing jobs and timber, clear-cutting sometimes destabilizes the soil surface and leads to mudslides, pollutes waterways, and destroys natural habitat and recreational forestland. Clear-cutting isn't the only form of harvest: today about 200,000 acres are selectively cut or salvage-harvested each year.

An Oregon Revised Statute calls for restrictions on clear-cut harvest along selected state and interstate highways where scenic vistas would be affected, thus creating a buffer of standing trees. Only those who have hiked an Oregon peak or flown over the state can see the total impact of clear-cuttings.

When you see a clear-cut forest, you are observing what was a battlefield between timber interests and conservationists—one where the trees lost.

PLOPPED IN THE MIDST OF THE IDYLLIC dairy farms, flanked by the fog-shrouded Coast Range and meandering rivers, the first sight of Blimp Hangar B is rather jarring. This is the world's largest clear-span wooden building, and huge letters spelling out AIR MUSEUM advertise its new use. Now the Tillamook Air Museum, the 1942 structure once housed a fleet of K-Class blimps used during World War II as ship escort and surveillance craft searching for Japanese submarines. These non-rigid airships escorted ship convoys from California to the San Juan Islands, and into and out of the Columbia River, the primary access to Kaiser shipbuilding yards in Portland and Vancouver. During the entire war, not one ship in a convoy escorted by a blimp was lost to a submarine attack.

Naval Air Station Tillamook and its two hangars (one burned in 1992) were among five such stations on the West Coast. With the steel shortage and abundance of Northwest timber, engineers decided to build seventeen hangars of predominately Douglas fir. This hangar is 1,072 feet long and could hold seven football fields side by side. About 3 million board feet of lumber was used to construct each of the Tillamook hangars, with an additional 7.5 million board feet for buildings in the compound at Tillamook.

Hangar B is a history-packed engineering marvel, and the first clear-span wooden structure of its size ever constructed. Fifty-one individual arched trusses were joined to form a gigantic rigid frame that was covered with 11.3 acres of roofing material. Two concrete towers positioned at either end of the hangar hold 180-ton doors.

Naval Air Station Tillamook was decommissioned in 1948. Of the eighty-four buildings, most were demolished or abandoned, but some were readapted to other uses. The Administrative Building and Men's Mess Hall have been restored, and the Blimp Hangar is now on the National Register of Historic Places. Of the seventeen wooden hangars constructed by the Navy in the United States, eight remain. Five were demolished, three were leveled by a hurricane, and Hangar A at Tillamook burned to the ground.

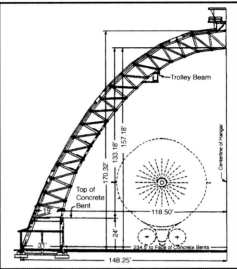

The arched truss was the key to the successful construction of the blimp hangars.

Details: Located 2 miles south of Tillamook off U.S. 101 at 6030 Hangar Rd., Tillamook Air Museum features WWII aircraft, a theater, and an interpretive room with photos and text explaining the construction and use of the blimp hangars. There is a great little café. Phone (503) 842-1130 or check out www.tillamookair.com.

Oregon Under Fire

Blimp Targets: Recently, declassified records from World War II confirm that blimps did more than escort ships and do reconnaissance. They were also involved in the sinking of two submarines off Cape Meares. If an enemy submarine surfaced, the blimp had the capacity to either sink it or direct surface vessels to the enemy sub. In late May 1943, two blimps dropped several depth charges on two submarines, which now lie on the ocean floor. One of the eight blimps at NAS Tillamook was stationed at Quillayute, Washington, each summer, where its mission was to intercept and destroy the balloon-delivered incendiary bombs launched by the Japanese.

Poopey Bags: That was the nickname for those reliable but not very sexy looking blimps. The K-Class "poopey bags" at NAS Tillamook were 252 feet long, with a control cabin about the size of a bus. The Goodyear blimp is 190 feet long.

Bomb over Brookings: In September 1942, a bomb was dropped from a Japanese Imperial Navy plane just north of Brookings Harbor. The claim to fame of the pilot, Nobuo Fujita, is that he represents the only foreign power to have dropped a bomb on the continental United States during the war. In 1992, the 50th anniversary of the bombing, Fujita planted a symbolic redwood on the spot where the bomb landed. There is also an on-site historical marker.

Subs off the Shoreline: The Imperial Japanese Navy outfitted eleven of their I-25 submarines to carry small seaplanes. The planes were used for reconnaissance but could also be armed. On June 21, 1942, a Japanese sub shelled the area around Fort Stevens near the mouth of the Columbia River. Fort Stevens, established during the Civil War, continued its purpose of protecting the entrance to the Columbia River until it was closed after World War II. It is now a state park and military museum (see. p. 8)

Balloon Bomb near Bly: See p. 85.

PAST THE MARINE DISCOVERY CENTER, Wax Work Museum and Arcade, and shops and restaurants of Newport's Bay Street is the most active fishing port on the Oregon coast. Three hundred commercial fishing boats moor amidst hundreds more pleasure craft.

It is 7 A.M. on a foggy Sunday morning as I stroll along the harbor trying to count the stacks of crab traps that turn the waterfront into a maze of metal and rope. The wind-ing walkway is new, benches line the land-scaped sidewalk, and the only sound comes from squawking gulls. Then I look down. Set into the sidewalk are tiles, and each one has a date, F/V with a name, and names of individuals. F/V stands for "fish-ing vessel," and the names and dates record fishermen dying or lost at sea. The walk begins at Dock 5 with the oldest docu-mented fatalities: 1920, Frances Gatens and Russ Kent (no name of the vessel).

The walkway project was a joint effort between the Port of Newport and the city financed by a grant to update the port's waterfront. The port's general manager, Don Mann, was throwing out some ideas with the architect when it was decided to dedicate the walkway to the fishermen. "The walkway is a constant reminder," said Mann. "It's very interesting to see people walk along with heads tucked; it's exciting to see them pay attention to it."

The local historical society worked on compiling names for a group of fishermen's wives who were involved with the Fishermen's Memorial Sanctuary at Yaquina State Park. The Memorial Walkway was dedicated on September 4, 2001, with 100 names set in tiles.

Details: Newport is on U.S. 101 at U.S. 20. The Memorial Walk is along the fishing docks north of the historic bayfront. The beaches, Yaquina Head Lighthouse, and tidepools all distinguish Newport, as do the 400 or so migrating gray whales off the shore. The region's most famous whale, Keiko, was the impetus behind con-struction of the Oregon Coast Aquarium in Newport. Even without the famous whale, who was moved from Newport and died in December 2003, the aquarium is a must-see.

Coastal Memorials

There are numerous memorials along the Oregon coast to those lost at seas. The following is a sampling.

Astoria: The Maritime Memorial honors not only fishermen who were lost but others involved in fishing: men and women who worked in canneries; the Coast Guard who supported the fishermen; and others whose life's work was on the river and sea. The semicircular granite wall faces the Columbia River, and the back of the monument opens to a small city park at the base of the Astoria-Megler Bridge. The memorial reads like a history text on the fishing industry: Judy Hogan, 1947–1993, Artist on the Bay; Alex Sarpola, 1856–1947, Gillnetter; Mollie A. Thompson, 1901–1999, Bumble Bee Line Lady; and on and on.

Hammond Boat Basin: At the point of the Hammond Boat Basin stands a large rock with a brass plate: "In memory of the valiant crew [of the] Coast Guard Motor Lifeboat TRIUMPH who on the night of Jan. 12, 1961 during a severe storm made the supreme sacrifice while assisting the fishing vessel Mermaid on Peacock Spit. 5 men lost."

LOST AT SEA

Charleston: An 8-foot bronze fisherman stands as a tribute to fishermen lost at sea: "To the sea they turned for life, / To the sea they gave their lives." The memorial, with seventy-five names as of press time, includes a small garden at the end of Kingfisher Drive off Boat Basin Drive.

Newport: "We wanted a place where names would be kept forever," explained Connie Kennedy. So Kennedy, along with other fishermen's wives, spearheaded a campaign to erect such a place; a decade later the Fishermen's Memorial Sanctuary at Yaquina State Park near Newport was dedicated. "It is a constant reminder."

Salmon Harbor, Winchester Bay: A red-and-white Coast Guard vessel sits dry-docked at Winchester Bay next to the Jack Unger Memorial Wayside. The weathered wood memorial reads: "The memorial is dedicated to the men & women from this port, who have been lost while seeking their livelihood from the sea." Jack Unger was not a fisherman but a mortician, community worker, and one-time

mayor who came to the Oregon coast in 1925. His passion was for the people of this fishing community and, according to his son, Jim, he dreamed of a pavilion overlooking the ocean to serve as a place for events and a memorial to those lost at sea. But Jack Unger died before his vision came to fruition. Locals wanted to honor him, so a fishermen's memorial was a natural monument to the man and the people he cared about.

Brookings: Next to the Chetco River Coast Guard Station at Brookings Harbor is a mariner's memorial dedicated to those who were lost in the horrific storm of August 16, 1972. The unexpected southerly equinox storm pummeled fishing vessels and sport boats, sinking five. Stars beside the names on the memorial indicate victims who were never recovered.

THERE ARE BEACH TOWNS, AND THEN there is Yachats (pronounced *Ya-hots*). This beach community seems stuck in a time warp. And that's not bad. Not that the Chamber of Commerce and local groups haven't tried to create tourist attractions, but with the spectacular scenery, sometimes it's best to leave it be—except for

Whale Park. The tiny park is sculpted into a lawn on U.S. 101 between Prospect Avenue and Yachats River Road in front of Bridgetown Espresso, which also happens to be Jabooka Bee Candle Company. I was standing on the shop's front porch when a light "rain" started falling. But there weren't any clouds in the sky, and the rain was

coming from the ground.

The sprinkling wasn't rain but spouting from a whale in the lawn, the town's only public park. The whale isn't always readily apparent...until it spouts.

Artist Jim Adler created this whale with steel-and-copper alloyed tail, grass-covered berm, and aforementioned spout. The shape of the berm and size of the tail are based on blueprints Adler obtained of a California gray whale, and the sculpture is the same size as the mammal.

According to Adler, the local Lions Club had donated the land to the city, and there were plans for a flagpole and veterans' memorial. Adler said to himself, "We can do better than that," and many of the townspeople agreed. The city finally gave permission for the artwork but wasn't ready to finance it, since, as Adler says, "It was art." But the city officials said, "Go ahead and raise the money." And Adler did. Actually, the artist says that the fundraising was the best part of the project since it brought people together, was a bunch of fun, and within three months the $18,000 for the project had been raised. For a town of 420 at the time, Adler pointed out, "That was quite an accomplishment."

The spout wasn't always a part of the sculpture plan; Adler jokingly suggested it to his wife, Ursula, who loved the idea. Adler built a mock-up of the sculpture to show the city commission, and that decided it. "The most fun was to wait for people on the commission I didn't like to lean over, and I'd hit the bulb."

> **Details:** Yachats is on U.S. 101 between Waldport and Florence. The park is on the east side of the highway between Prospect and Yachats River Road.

What a Dish

What a Dish: OK, so it's not real art, rather a bit of innovative recycling. A circular pond is the centerpiece of a small garden on the grounds of Joe and Joette's Town Center Café and Bakery on the west side of U.S. 101 in Yachats. The pond is really a satellite dish that retired art gallery owner and super volunteer Bernie Church painted green, surrounded with rocks and plantings and, voilà, a satellite garden. "There's nothing on TV," explained Church in his Australian accent. "I'm back into reading, so this is just recycling."

Little Log Church: Then there's the more traditional sort of landmark, the 1930, cross-shaped, timber church that now serves as the Yachats Historical Museum.

HEADING NORTH ALONG U.S. 101 FROM northern California into Oregon, you begin to notice a change in the roadside gift shops. Stores full of redwood burl—everything from kitschy clocks to coffee tables—evolve into Oregon myrtlewood "factories." By the time you reach the Wooden Nickel in Port Orford, you're probably curious. What's Oregon myrtlewood, and are these really factories?

Oregon woodworkers have created a small cottage industry using the tree found only in this region. Each factory along the highway usually features woodworkers who have carved out a special niche for themselves. Once there were close to fifty retail outlets; today there are three large factories, half a dozen smaller production shops, and around thirty outlets in the southern coastal range. This is the myrtlewood belt and home of *Umbellularia californica*—also commonly known as California laurel and bay laurel.

Myrtlewood aficionados like to quote biblical references to myrtle and conclude that the same tree grows in the Holy Land: "And instead of the briar shall come up the myrtle tree" (Isaiah 55:13). Not exactly. Oregon myrtlewood sprouts from the Lauraceae family while the myrtle tree of Holy Land fame is of the Myrtaceae family.

Myrtlewood is a broadleaf evergreen with wood 20 percent harder than maple. When crushed, the leaves produce a strong camphor-like odor, and legend has it that the Hudson's Bay trappers used it to brew a medicinal tea.

Since it's so slow growing, myrtlewood's grain is affected by various soil conditions and bacteria—resulting in swirling burls, sapsucker leaves, and trunks and branches that separate then reunite. Most of the really strange formations grow near a tree's base. Over a few hundred years' growth, this creates dramatic grain patterns and colors, producing some of the greatest variation among American woods. Trees used for woodworking are 150–300 years old, and today most are found in forests about to be clear-cut. Standing alone, a single tree looks like a gigantic, perfectly pruned shrub. In a forest it becomes lankier as the branches grow 40–70 feet reaching for the sun.

Watching the transformation from tree to bowl makes for an interesting stop. The Myrtlewood Factory, between Reedsport and North Bend, is the granddaddy of myrtlewood factories, established in 1911. Owner Bob Gales personally shows guests through the facility pointing out each step,

from the rough milling of the logs to the kiln drying, then onto the lathe, and finally sanding and finishing of each piece. Not a single piece looks the same; this is not your typical assembly-line operation.

Myrtlewood was used for shipbuilding and furniture making before it became the fancy of woodworkers creating bowls, gavels, and wineglasses. Out of respect for the deceased tree, avoid the tacky souvenirs. Some of the pieces are true works of art.

Details: Myrtlewood Factory is 5 miles north of North Bend and is one of half a dozen factories offering tours; call (541) 756-2220.

Living Oregon Myrtlewood

Inland off Oregon 42 between Coquille and Myrtle Point is Coquille Myrtle Grove State Natural Site, where you can picnic among the trees. The best place to see a perfect specimen is the town of Myrtle Point, once the site of an entire grove. Pick up a Tree Trail brochure at the dome-shaped Coos County Logging Museum (originally a church) at Maple and 7th. An easy-to-see premier myrtle grows by the Myrtle Point High School football field at Harris and 6th.

ON FEBRUARY 4, 1999, THE JAPANESE-owned freighter NM/V *New Carissa* ran aground 150 yards off the sandy spit near Coos Bay. On board was a crew of twenty-three, its cargo of wood chips, and 400,000 gallons of bunker oil. The crew was rescued, but as the storm pounded the ship the tar-like oil began leaking. While the storm began tearing the ship apart, a removal operation that included pumping, burning, towing, firebombing, torpedoing, and exploding napalm ensued in one of the most bizarre rescue efforts in modern maritime history.

After failed attempts to burn the trapped fuel from the ship as it lurched on a shifting sandbar, the *New Carissa* broke into two sections, spilling about 70,000 gallons of thick oil. Tugboat *Sea Victory* was called on to brave the weather and attempt to tow the *New Carissa*'s 440-foot bow section out to sea where it would be sunk. First, crews and salvage officials began pumping fuel from the tanks.

Pumping operations were abandoned as hail and winds battered the rescue workers, lines kinked, and oil spilled into the sea. The following day, *Sea Victory* began towing the hulking bow out to sea; at about 40 miles out, the towline snapped in a fierce Pacific storm, and the bow free-floated through tumultuous seas, finally beaching near Waldport where it again leaked oil.

Finally, on March 11, the bow was towed out to sea, but sinking it was another matter. Remote-controlled explosive charges failed to sink the ship, so the big guns were called in to finish the job. The destroyer U.S.S. *David R. Ray* barraged the ship with artillery fire, then the nuclear sub U.S.S. *Bremerton* fired a torpedo into the hull. Two hours later, the ship that had humiliated and baffled hundreds of maritime professionals slipped below the waves to be buried at sea. "It had nine lives and it was not willing to cooperate with us. This thing seems to have a life of its own," said Navy Comdr. Cliff Perkins, the destroyer's commanding officer to the press.

Millions of dollars and multiple pending lawsuits later, the stern section of the *New Carissa* remains firmly implanted on the North Spit of Coos Bay.

Details: Heading north on U.S. 101, cross the McCullough Bridge in Coos Bay, turn left on the Horsfall Beach road (Power Rd.), and follow the road 4.4 miles just past the North Spit Boat Ramp. A one-lane, sand road accessed only by four-wheel drive or on foot is to the right. Two miles down the spit and over the dune is what's left of the *New Carissa*…looking about as old as the *Peter Iredale* wreck (see. p. 8).

AS IN DOZENS OF OREGON'S COASTAL communities, the economy of Bandon has evolved from timber to fishing to tourism. But Bandon, with its stunning shoreline of sea stacks and miles of sandy beaches, is

more than a historic tourist town with swanky golf courses. It is the Cranberry Capital of the West Coast. And come October, the cranberry harvest is in full swing. To prepare for the harvest, Bandon has come up with a September Cranberry Festival with a blessing of the harvest, street fair, queen, parade, Lions Club barbeque, and golf tournament. Cranberries offer a colorful excuse for a party.

Faber Farms is one of about 170 cranberry farms in southern Oregon. Faber dedicates 51 acres of its 200-acre farm to cranberries. The fields are partitioned into 2-acre plots, each surrounded by earth dikes. The ground inside has been excavated, with a crown in the center for drainage. A layer of peat followed by a foot of sand ready the field for planting. Vines, 6–8-inch cuttings, are planted into the sand, which holds the fine hair roots of developing plants. The vines flower each season when bees are brought in to pollinate.

The vines grow for 3 years before the first harvest, but they don't reach full maturity for 6 or 7 years. The tenacious plants continue to produce cranberries for decades—the earliest known vines in the region were planted in the late nineteenth century.

When the fields are ready for harvest, they are flooded to cover the vines. A "beater" drives over the flooded field and bars rotating on a reel knock the berries from the vine. The fruit floats to the surface, creating the picture-perfect cranberry bog. Boom boards skim across the water collecting the fruit, which is then pumped

from the bog. The berries are cleaned, sorted, and packed in 1,200-pound containers and shipped to the processor. Water from the first flooded field is drained into the next, and the process is repeated. Each field takes two days to harvest: a day to flood, a day to beat and pull off the fruit. These cranberries are then sold for juice and sauce. The cranberries found in the produce section of your grocery store are dry-harvested: a harvester walks behind a picker that combs through the vines harvesting the fruit.

Oregon cranberry growers think their product surpasses the East Coast variety since they leave the berries on the vine until they are ripe, making them higher in sugar, darker in color, and lower in acid.

Details: Faber Farms, 54982 Morrison Rd. off Oregon 42, offers tours Monday through Saturday. For further information, call (541) 347-1166 or check out www.faberfarms.com.

Cranberry Factoids

That's a Bunch of Berries: According to the Oregon Agricultural Statistics Service, 30 million pounds of cranberries were harvested in the state in 2002.

We Try Harder: Oregon ranks fourth in U.S. cranberry production, just ahead of Washington and behind Wisconsin, Massachusetts, and New Jersey. Oregon ranks second behind Wisconsin for cranberry yield per acre.

It's the Climate: Sandy, acidic soils combined with the area's climate make cranberries one of the few agricultural commodities that can excel along the strip of coast from Coos Bay to Port Orford.

THE HEADLAND OF CAPE ARAGO HOOKS into the Pacific, and from the scenic overlook you have a box seat with a full view of one of Mother Nature's orchestra pits. Below the overlook is Shell Island and Simpson Reef, where seals and sea lions haul themselves out of the Pacific to display, lounge, molt, breed, or bask—showing the varying shades of their plush gray or brown beauty. When the sounds of breaking waves and barking California sea lions come together, they create the percussion section of this particular symphony. The noise is deafening, the beauty astounding.

With its softly sloping beaches and offshore rocks, this area serves as the prime location on the Oregon coast for Steller sea lions, California sea lions, northern elephant seals, and harbor seals to hoist themselves to solid ground. The only time elephant seals come to land is to breed and molt, and since 1993 the winter breeders have hauled out here. Females, weighing up to 1,000 pounds, produce one pup, which must survive the crashing waves for 8–10 weeks before it can swim on its own.

Typically six to ten pups are born here each year; only in one calm year were any pups known to have survived.

Harbor seals give birth March through May, and their pups can swim at birth. Steller sea lions haul out at Simpson Reef year round. Male California sea lions leave the females and pups in California, head north and haul out here—sort of pinniped boys' night out.

Simpson Reef and Shell Island are two of 1,400 rocks, reefs, islands, and headlands designated Oregon Islands National Wildlife

Refuge sites. In addition to pinnipeds, gray whales migrate along the coast, and thirteen species of seabirds nest here, including pelagic and double-crested cormorants, murres, tufted puffins, Leach's and fork-tailed storm petrels, and rhinoceros auklets. There are dozens of hiking trails and lookouts from the mainland, but all of these coastal rocks and islands are closed to public access to protect the birds and pinnipeds from their greatest enemy, humans.

Details: Simpson Reef Interpretive Overlook is located at Cape Arago State Park, south of Charleston and Sunset Bay on Cape Arago Highway between Shore Acres and Cape Arago. Shoreline Education for Awareness docents are on hand from 10 A.M. to 4 P.M. on weekends from May through September. Spotting scopes are available for viewings, so bring plenty of quarters! Special arrangements can be made to meet docents by calling (541) 347-3683.

"SHORE ACRES"

Shore Acres

One of the Oregon coast's great surprises is Shore Acres State Park. The former summer estate of lumber baron and shipbuilder Louis Simpson, Shore Acres' five acres of

landscaped formal gardens offer a striking contrast to the rugged coastal beauty. Plants from around the world fill the grounds, which are maintained jointly by Oregon State Parks and the Friends of Shore Acres. The gardens offer seasonal plantings beginning with hundreds of spring bulbs from late February through March; 5,000 tulips in late March through April; hundreds of rhododendrons and azaleas April through mid-May; 5,000 flowering annuals and perennials through the summer along with 900 rose bushes; dahlias blooming through mid-October, just in time for workers to string the holiday lights that glow from Thanksgiving through New Year's.

The original Simpson estate burned in 1921, and the second mansion (pictured above) was eventually razed after the estate was purchased by the state for use as a

public park in 1942. There is an observation building where the mansion once stood.

THE *TYRANNOSAURUS REX* STANDS guard in front of the Prehistoric Gardens south of Port Orford. Anyone with a car full of kids numbed by the natural beauty of the coast and ready for a little kitsch can't help but enjoy E. V. Nelson's lifelong passion.

Long before *Jurassic Park* made dinosaurs part of pop culture, Mr. Nelson was creating lifelike, full-scale brachiosaurs, triceratops, dimetrodons, and trachodons. For 40 years the sculptor worked on the beasts from "The Land of Long Ago." What makes them so creepy fun is the drippy ferns, layers of moss, and towering trees in this genuine temperate rain forest where the prehistoric wanna-bes make their home. The flora is as gigantic as the beasts; the area gets an average of 6.5 feet of rain each year. In addition to the dinos are storyboards detailing infor-mation about the beasts, plants, and forests placed along the weaving walkways.

Mr. Nelson died in 1999; family members continue operating the Prehistoric Gardens.

Details: The Prehistoric Gardens, between Gold Beach and Port Orford on U.S. 101, is open every day of the year. (541) 332-4463.

TRAVELERS ON U.S. 101 ALONG THE coast will no doubt notice a variety of bright blue-and-white signs with a snarling tsunami wave. Some note Tsunami Hazard Zones while others indicate Tsunami Evacuation Routes or Sites. Hmmmm, you might ask yourself as you eye the stunning shoreline pocked with rock formations, eroded cliffs, and curling, crashing waves: What's a tsunami and should I worry about it?

Tsunamis are big, and we do mean BIG, waves caused by the uplift of the sea floor during an earthquake as well as by landslides and volcanic undersea eruptions. During the past 204 years, twenty-four tsunamis have caused damage and death in the United States and its territories. Hawaii, Alaska, Washington, Oregon, and California have all suffered destruction from tsunamis. Studies show that the Oregon coast is vulnerable to tsunamis caused by offshore earthquakes in the Cascadia Subduction Zone fault system that runs from British Columbia to Northern California.

There are two kinds of tsunamis for Oregonians to think about: local and distant. Local earthquakes along the Cascadia Subduction Zone generate tsunamis that can strike the southern Oregon coast in 10–15 minutes and the northern coast in 20–30 minutes. The warning system is the earthquake itself. The last local earthquake and tsunami off the Oregon coast hit about 300 years ago, and scientists speculate that there is a 10–20 percent chance of a recurrence in the next 50 years. While these tsunamis are rare, they are deadly.

For Oregon, distant tsunamis are caused by undersea earthquakes anywhere in the Pacific Rim outside the Cascadia, and they take several hours to reach the Oregon coast. The most recent distant tsunami was in 1964, when a 9.2 quake hit the coast of Alaska, then made a treacherous trek down the Pacific coast, where it killed four people at Beverly Beach and ravaged many coastal communities.

In 1995 the Oregon legislature passed a bill that limited construction of new essential facilities, such as fire stations, and special occupancy structures, such as schools, in tsunami flooding zones. The Oregon Department of Geology and Mineral Industries and Oregon Emergency Management, along with other state and local agencies, set to work with coastal communities to identify these zones, educate the public of their hazards, and plan evacuation routes. The gist of tsunami evacuation is to head for high ground immediately after the shaking stops (that explains the figure on the Tsunami Hazard Zone sign running uphill with a menacing wave behind him)! If you grew up during the Cold War with duck-and-cover drills in your school, you'd be right at home on the coast, since public schools in coastal communities are required to hold tsunami evacuation as well as drop-cover-and-hold earthquake drills every year.

By the late 1990s, Tsunami Hazard and Evacuation Route signs were being installed along the Oregon coast. Oregon's Travel and Information Council installed tsunami informational markers in Seaside, Newport, and Reedsport in 1995. Recently, sets of Tsunami Hazard Zone signs were being placed at each end of designated stretches along U.S. 101 in a cooperative effort involving individual communities, Oregon Emergency Management, the Oregon Department of Transportation, and the Department of Geology and Mineral Industries.

Coastal earthquakes and tsunamis are just two of the geological occurrences that continually shape and recreate the remarkable Oregon coast.

> **Details:** For more information on tsunamis and other natural hazards of Oregon, check out these sites: www.oregongeology.com and www.naturenw.org.

Willamette Valley

To appreciate the beauty and bounty of Oregon's heartland, you must turn off the paved backbone of Interstate 5. On the highways and back roads you'll find rolling fields of flowers, Christmas tree farms, thriving vineyards and intimate wineries, thirty-four covered bridges, the state capital, and small towns with roots in timber and agriculture. The state's two major universities carry on the business of higher education and rivalry in the Willamette Valley, where famous authors and athletes have made their names.

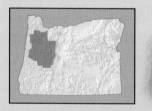

1 Good Pasture Bridge
2 Ken Kesey Memorial, Pre's Rock, Home of the U of O Ducks
3 Monaco Coach
4 Home of the OSU Beavers
5 State Hospital and State Capitol
6 Silver Falls State Park
7 Gordon House, Oregon Garden
8 Yamhill Wine Country

Crimson clover, near Monroe

WHERE THERE IS WATER, THERE ARE bridges. In Oregon, historic covered bridges offer not only access from one side of a river or creek to the other but a link to the state's past.

The Good Pasture Bridge—the state's longest covered bridge still in daily use—spans the McKenzie River off Oregon Highway 126 just east of Vida in Lane County. It is a one-way, 165-foot-long, creaking wooden bit of time travel. The classical architecture, Gothic-style windows, arched portal, and pitched roof make it one of the loveliest and most photographed covered bridges in the state. Built in 1938 at a cost of $13,154, this is not just a tourist stop. Logging trucks cross the span daily. Loads like that take their toll, so in 1987 Lane County repaired and renovated Good Pasture Bridge. This time the job cost $750,000.

Let's Cover the Subject

County with the Most Covered Bridges: Lane County, home of Good Pasture, Belknap, Chambers Railroad, Coyote Creek, Currin, Deadwood, Dorena, Earnest, Lowell, Mosby Creek, Nelson Mountain, Office, Parvin, Pengra, Steward, Unity, Wendling, and Wildcat covered bridges.

Oldest Covered Bridge: Drift Creek Bridge in Lincoln County might be the oldest covered bridge (1914), but no one really knows. Not only that, but the bridge was removed from its original location in 1997 and is being reconstructed on private property near Otis. The 1917 Gallon House Bridge spanning Abiqua Creek is one of the oldest in the state and the only remaining covered bridge in Marion County.

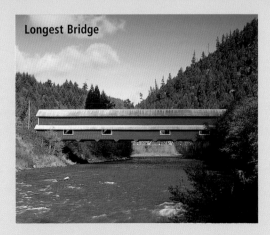

Longest Bridge

Shortest Covered Bridge: Neal Bridge over South Myrtle Creek in Douglas County measures 42 feet in length.

Most Dubious Name: Locals say Gallon House Bridge over Abique Creek got its name during prohibition from a liquor dispensary that operated at the north end. Then there's Short Bridge. At 105 feet it's not considered short; rather, it was renamed from the original Whiskey Butte Bridge to Short Bridge after area resident Gordon Short.

Most Viewed: Grave Creek Bridge in Josephine County can be seen from Interstate 5, about 15 miles north of Grants Pass.

Longest Bridge: The 180-foot Office Bridge over the Middle Fork of the Willamette River was constructed by the Westfir Lumber Company in 1944 with triple trusses to support logging trucks. It is closed to the public.

KEN KESEY'S LIFE AND WORK SO permeated Oregon that one may not realize that the author, counterculture hero, Merry Prankster, social commentator, father, jailbird, teacher, guru of psychedelic drugs, and cultural icon didn't sprout from the fog-shrouded environs he loved and so often wrote about.

Mr. Kesey was born in La Junta, Colorado, on September 17, 1935. On November 10, 2001, he died in Eugene. "We've lost our Merry Prankster," the obituary began in Eugene's *Register-Guard.*

During his 66 years, the author's fame spread as quickly as the counterculture he espoused. Young Kesey moved to Coburg, Oregon, in 1943 and was raised near Springfield. Born into a family of great outdoors lovers, he explored, hunted, and fished. He attended Springfield Junior High, where he met Faye Haxby, who would become his wife. "My first period class was art and Ken's was drama. I was painting sets for the play he was rehearsing. My first hour of school in Springfield, I met him," recalled Mrs. Kesey.

At Springfield High, Ken was a star wrestler and football player with a passion for drama. Voted Most Talented by his peers, he graduated in 1953. He enrolled at the

University of Oregon; Faye went to Oregon State; they were married midway through their college work. Ken graduated with a degree in speech and drama, but with an eye on writing. Before attending Stanford University, he took a year off to write a novel. "By the time he finished it, he knew he didn't want to publish it," explained Mrs. Kesey. At Stanford he met and worked with Richard Snowcroft and Wallace Stegner, but Mrs. Kesey says his love of literature was nurtured at the U of O.

But other adventures lured him away, and he dropped out and began experimenting with drugs. In Menlo Park, California, Ken volunteered to be an experimental drug subject, then took a job at a mental hospital. It was there that the inspiration for his first published novel, *One Flew Over the Cuckoo's Nest,* was born. The ground-breaking 1962 novel was made into a movie filmed at Oregon State Mental Hospital in Salem. The film won five Academy Awards, yet Kesey never saw it. His second novel, *Sometimes a Great Notion,* was set in an Oregon logging town; the cinema version was filmed near Depoe Bay. *Last Go Around* was an account of an Oregon rodeo rivalry and the 1911 Pendleton Round-Up he cowrote with Ken Babbs in 1994. The descriptions

of Oregon in his writing are both lovingly descriptive and hauntingly ominous.

As one of the Merry Pranksters, he traveled around the country in the Day-Glo–painted bus "Further." In 1965 he was arrested for possession of marijuana and served five months in the San Mateo county jail. There he wrote and illustrated *Kesey's Jail Journal,* which was published on the second anniversary of his death. Kesey returned to Oregon in 1967, moved to a farm in Pleasant Hill with Faye and their three children, taught a writing seminar at the U of O, became a community activist, lectured, and returned to writing, including *Little Trick the Squirrel Meets Big Double Bear,* one of two children's book, dozens of articles, plays, and journals—although never with the scope of his two great novels.

On November 14, 2001, the Eugene community bid farewell to Ken Kesey at the 750-seat McDonald Theater, where hundreds overflowed onto the streets and listened to Dave Frohmayer, president of the University of Oregon, Ken Babbs, and others talk about their friend while Mason Williams played music. Strains of "And We Bid You Good Night," by the Grateful Dead did just that. Friends, many in their 60s, spent three days digging the grave for Kesey's swirling paint-patterned coffin in a field on his farm. On Friday, November 16, Ken Kesey was buried next to his son Jed.

On the second anniversary of Kesey's death, a life-size statue created by sculptor Peter Helzer was unveiled in downtown Eugene at the corner of Willamette and Broadway. It shows Kesey reading to his three grandchildren. At the dedication, Faye Kesey sat on the bench next to the statue: "My arm just fell on his shoulder as it would naturally. It felt just right."

WE ARE TALKING ABOUT A COUPLE OF fine schools: the University of Oregon and Oregon State University—the first in Eugene, the latter in Corvallis. One is known for its liberal arts education, the other's roots are in agriculture. But let's get right to the heart of things: the schools' mascots.

Ducks

Once upon a time, around 1876 when the University of Oregon was founded, the school's students acquired the nickname Webfoots—not in honor of the dripping wet environment or ducks, but for a group of fishermen from the coast of Massachusetts whose descendents settled in Oregon's Willamette Valley. Sports writers, erroneously thinking webfoot meant duck's feet, started calling the school's teams Ducks. That prompted students to bring a white duck named Puddles to sports events. Puddles was ducky, but not practical.

© Disney

Around 1943, cartoons featuring Puddles began to appear in a student publication. Puddles had a startling resemblance to Walt Disney's Donald Duck. In 1947, Disney studios contacted the University about the similarity between the U of O's Duck mascot and Donald Duck. Officials from the University met with Walt Disney in Anaheim, California, and an informal agreement was reached granting the university permission to use the Donald look-alike as its sports mascot. A contract was put in place in 1975 formalizing the rights to use the Duck as the University's sports mascot. The understanding continued swimmingly until 1990, when the University and Disney

Enterprises negotiated an agreement by which the University can enter into trademark licensing agreements allowing for the use of the Duck on T-shirts and other officially licensed products. The University of Oregon and Disney Enterprises, Inc., agreement is unique in college licensing and the Duck well loved by its flock.

As for the yellow and green colors, the screaming (or officially noted lightning) yellow was adopted with green for the 2003 football season as part of the new Nike-designed uniforms and accompanying ad campaign. A wonderful reason to purchase all new Duck-fan-correct attire.

It is believed by the author that the Oregon Duck is the only NCAA mascot that arrives on the football field on the back of a roaring motorcycle.

Beavers

First off, OSU's official colors aren't orange and black. Nope, originally the very staid navy and white served as the school colors, and when that changed in 1893, the color (singular) was orange. The sports teams were dubbed Orangemen or Aggies. While black was never officially adopted, it has been the background color since orange bumped navy and white.

As for Benny the Beaver, whoa. The first mascot was a coyote named Jimmie. Nothing special there, but the most famous OSU mascot was local Presbyterian minister and member of the OSU Board of Regents John Robert Newton Bell, who served as the school's living mascot from 1893 to 1928—

not a little white duck named Puddles. Reverend Bell's favorite tradition was to parade students and faculty to Mary's River after a Civil War game (that's the annual U of O vs. OSU football rivalry), where he would toss his hat into the river to symbolize "burying the lemon-yellow."

The first reference to Beavers as the mascot was either 1910 or 1911. Whatever the exact year, there was some competition over who was the official mascot—Reverend Bell or a Beaver. References to a live beaver named Billy and a cartoon rendition flourished from 1933 to 1944 according to George Edmonston Jr., writing for the *Oregon Stater* campus newspaper. Benny Beaver officially became OSU's mascot in 1945. This was handy, since the official Oregon state animal is a beaver.

In 1951 the first student donned a Benny Beaver costume and showed up at sports events. In the 1980s to the mid-1990s, in step with the times, Benny was joined by Bernice, a female beaver mascot, giving OSU the distinction of having the only male and female mascots in the NCAA. Benny and Bernice wore wedding attire each Homecoming Game.

Cartoonish gentle Benny was the official and much loved mascot until early 2001, when he was replaced with the fierce "angry" Beaver of today. The Office of University Advancement announced that the adoption of the new "angry" Beaver logo was meant to give OSU football a new more aggressive image. This says something, I'm not sure what, about the evolution of college sports.

STEVE PREFONTAINE RAN HARD AND died young. On May 30, 1975, on Skyline Road near Hendricks Park, the University of Oregon's premiere distance runner, Steve Prefontaine, missed a turn, hit a rock, and rolled his MGB in a one-car accident that took his life.

The rock where Pre died became a pilgrimage for other runners and fans, who continue to be drawn here not only by his talent on the track but by his charisma. "PRE 5-30-75 R.I.P." is painted in white on the rock. A permanent memorial was erected nearby. It reads:

> *"PRE"*
> *For your dedication and loyalty*
> *To your principles and beliefs,*
> *For your love, warmth, and friendship,*
> *For your family and friends...*
> *You are missed by so many,*
> *And you will never be forgotten...*

At the time of his death at age 24, the Coos Bay native and hometown hero had achieved international star status in the world of track and field. His accomplishments included every American running record between 2,000 and 10,000 meters and between 2 and 6 miles, and a fourth place medal in the 1972 Munich Olympics. U of O fans chanted when he appeared at Hayward Field, and he never disappointed; Prefontaine never lost a race at Hayward Field. "How can you lose with 12,000 people behind you?" he once commented.

Steve was the first athlete to win four consecutive NCAA track titles in the same

Pre's Oregon Trail

Coos Bay: Steve Prefontaine was born here and attended Marshall High School, where he began setting state records before being recruited by coach Bill Bowerman to run for the University of Oregon. Each September the Prefontaine Memorial Run, a 10K road race across his old training courses, finishes at the high school track where he first competed. The Coos Bay hometown hero returned to Pirates Field at Marshall High for the last time at his funeral. The Steve Prefontaine Track was dedicated in his honor in 2001. The Coos Art Museum in downtown Coos Bay showcases Prefontaine's career with a permanent exhibit of his trophies, awards, photographs, artwork, and memorabilia. A memorial and plaque listing Prefontaine's track records also stands downtown near the visitor center.

Book: *Pre: The Story of America's Greatest Running Legend, Steve Prefontaine,* by Tom Jordan.

Film Legacy: Two unrelated movies featuring the short life of Steve Prefontaine are available on video. The superior *Without Limits* stars Billy Crudup as Prefontaine and Donald Sutherland as his coach, Bill Bowerman; *Prefontaine* was released by Disney. Additionally, the 1995 documentary *Fire on the Track* continues to inspire runners.

The Prefontaine Classic: This premiere track and field event has been held each May at the U of O's Hayward Field since 1974. Athletes must be ranked in the top fifty in the world in their event to be eligible to complete in this showcase meet.

Nike: Steve Prefontaine was the first runner to wear what would become a Nike running shoe. Then he became the first person to market Nike shoes to other runners. Today, at Nike corporate headquarters in Beaverton there is a Prefontaine building with a statue of Pre standing in the middle of the corporate campus.

event. On fourteen different occasions he broke his own and other American records. At the age of 19 he was a cover boy for *Sports Illustrated*. Pre, as his fans and friends called him, made running cool.

Medals, ribbons, and flowers continue to be left by those inspired by Steve Prefontaine, many of whom were not yet born when he lost his life. On January 25, 2001, Steve Prefontaine would have been 50 years old. *Eugene Register-Guard* columnist Ron Bellamy wrote this for the occasion: "How remarkable, for an athlete to have had

such an impact in life, as America's greatest distance runner, and to continue to have an impact a quarter-century later. It wasn't just the races he won, but how he won them, never giving anything less than all.... It wasn't just what he did, but what he stood for, the rights of athletes and the highest ideals of his sport."

Details: Hayward Field is between E. 15th Ave. and E. 18th Ave. on Agate St. The Bowerman statue stands in front of Bowerman Building on E. 15th.

Coach Bill Bowerman

There wouldn't be one without the other. Or at least, they wouldn't have been the same men. Bill Bowerman, the University of Oregon's track and field coach for 24 years, coached dozens of winning athletes, but the most famous was distance runner Steve Prefontaine.

Coach Bowerman recruited Prefontaine in 1969, and when Pre accepted the offer Bowerman wrote the community of Coos Bay a "thank you" note expressing his gratitude for the part they played in supporting their favorite son. Bowerman's coaching would have made him famous, but his invention of the waffle sole on what became the Nike running shoe is what made him rich. Bowerman, in search of a lightweight shoe with traction, created the "waffle shoe" for Steve Prefontaine using his wife's waffle iron. He patented eight athletic shoe designs and, with Phil Knight, was cofounder of Nike.

Bowerman was an inspiration to more than his team and the U of O family. He became an avid jogger and cowrote the booklet *Jogging* for ordinary runners. Bowerman died in December 1999.

A life-size statue designed by former Nike artist Diana Lee Jackson stands outside the Bowerman Building next to Hayward Field, where he seems to be studying the track. The inscription reads:

Bill Bowerman
Teacher, Innovator
Visionary, Motivator
*   And then there was the waffle iron.*

The statue is mounted on waffle irons.

THE U.S. PRESIDENT MAY HAVE THE Boeing 747-200B jets at his disposal, but in Oregon the governor has access to the Beaver Patriot, a 40-foot rolling office produced by Monaco Coach Corporation and outfitted with technology by Intel. Call it Air Force One of the Oregon highways.

In November 2003, Governor Ted Kulongoski, among other officials, acquired use of the 30,000-pound coach à la office on six wheels on loan through the Associated Oregon Industries lobby and Monaco Coach. Called Connecting Oregon, not only does the deal give the governor mobile digs, but it showcases Oregon's enterprise and industry as it cruises across the state with sponsor insignias decorating the exterior. Sort of a NASCAR approach to the state's businesses.

Monaco Coach Corporation is one of three motor coach and RV companies in Lane County, making this a mecca of motor coaches. Monaco Coach produces a line of custom RVs and motor coaches at its 2.5-million-square-foot plant off Interstate 5 in Coburg just north of Eugene. This is Monaco's headquarters, but they have other production facilities in Bend, Oregon, and in Indiana. Monaco employs up to 3,500 workers in Coburg, ranking it among the top five employers in Lane County.

Marathon Coach Incorporated has been converting commercial buses into luxury recreational vehicles and corporate coaches since 1983, and in 1994 it moved into its custom-built 134,000-square-foot production facility also off Interstate 5 in Coburg. Marathon employs about 375 people in the bus-conversion production plant.

Country Coach, in Junction City, northwest of Coburg on Oregon Highway 99, produces a line of motor coaches and RVs, employs 1,000 folks, and is among the county's top ten employers, according to the Lane County Council of Governments' 2002 figures.

> **Details:** Monaco Coach, 91320 Coburg Industrial Way, (541) 686-8011; tours 10 A.M. and 2 P.M., Monday through Friday; Marathon Coach, also on Coburg Industrial Way, tours 11:30 A.M., Monday through Friday; Country Coach, 210 E. 6th Ave., Junction City, tours 9 A.M. and 1:30 P.M., Monday through Thursday excluding holidays; reservations are requested, by calling (800) 654-0223.

OREGON STATE HOSPITAL SPREADS over 148 acres of lawns and gardens, with historic and new buildings occasionally wrapped with chain-link fence topped with coiled barbed wire, giving the impression of a high-security college campus—without students.

The compound banks both sides of Center Street about 8 miles east of the state capitol. On the south side of Center stands J Building. Dedicated in 1883, the first of forty-eight buildings in what was the Oregon State Insane Asylum, it was constructed by convict labor from the neighboring state penitentiary. The first 261 male patients were transferred from Portland's Hawthorne Asylum, followed by 102 female patients under the supervision of the state's first asylum director, Dr. Horace Carpenter. Patient population continued to grow until it peaked in 1958 with 3,545 patients, then declined as deinstitutionalization became popular.

The 1912 Dome Building on the other side of Center Street, now the Administration Building, stands as a landmark for another reason. Here the screen adaptation of Ken Kesey's *One Flew Over the Cuckoo's Nest* was filmed, using patients and staff in their real-life roles and giving new meaning to "cameo appearance." The idea of asking patients and staff to take part in the project was the brainchild of the hospital superintendent, Dean R. Brooks, who played himself in the film. Dr. Brooks saw the experience as an exercise in therapy. The film garnered five Academy Awards and brought mental health to the forefront of public awareness when it came out in 1975.

On the west side of the hospital grounds is Memorial Circle, where the ashes of those who died at the state hospital, if not claimed by a friend or relative, are laid to rest. In 1910 a crematory was constructed, and all bodies in the asylum's cemetery (site of the Dome building) were deinterred, cremated, and buried in what is now Memorial Circle.

Details: Oregon State Hospital, 2600 Center St. NE., Salem.

THE MODERN GREEK–STYLE CAPITOL in Salem stands as Oregon's third try at a building to house state government. Two previous statehouses were lost to fire, one in 1855 and the other in 1935; both structures followed conventional architectural designs of the time. The current four-story capitol was completed in 1938, with two wings added in 1977.

Some call the capitol bland, others equate it to a gigantic tiered wedding cake, but the stark white Vermont marble exterior and the building's grounds are chock full of surprises—none quite as visible as the Golden Pioneer atop the tower, who surveys the surrounding city, rolling hills, farmland, and forests. While that gold-leafed guy might seem more appropriate in the Golden State (that would be California), he is meant to represent the pioneers and the pioneer spirit that cleared, settled, farmed, and logged the state of Oregon. The statue's official moniker is Oregon Pioneer, so-named by its creator, artist Ulric H. Ellerhusen.

OK, so some just call him the Little Fellow, but the Pioneer is far from small. The statue is 23 feet high with a bronze body that weighs 8.5 tons. Ellerhusen cast the figure in his New Jersey studio, then it was shipped through the Panama Canal, traveled by railroad car to Salem, and was delivered on a flatbed truck. The Golden Pioneer was losing its luster and was regilded in 1958 and again in 1984. You can get up close and personal with the statue by climbing 121 steps to the Observation Deck that encircles the base of the Pioneer.

At night, the statue is bathed in light generated from solar panels, making Oregon the first state in the nation to use renewable energy to light its capitol. Engineering professionals volunteered their services, and on Earth Day, April 22, 2002, the solar panels were lifted into place on the building's west roof.

Ellerhusen also sculpted five marble relief works for the exterior of the building and the state seal for the 106-foot-high rotunda. Two marble sculptures by Leo Friedlander of a covered wagon and Lewis and Clark led by Sacagawea flank the main entrance. Inside, stunning murals and paintings covering the walls and rotunda tell the state's history and economy.

Don't skip the mall grounds. The Columbus Day storm of 1964 uprooted many of the early plantings, but the landscape is full of ornamental and native trees and flowers and more statues and contemporary artwork. The pavers along the main promenade are purely Oregon-odd. Architect Bart Guthrie selected quotes or folklore from the collection of state historian Cecil Edwards for each paver. They run from the hilarious to serious:

1934
Dead Broke
Oregon is dead broke.
—Gov. Julius Meier, Reporting to Oregon during the Great Depression

In Manzanita people don't mind what you do, so long as they know about it.
—Anonymous

1918 National Guard
Portland National Guard
First in the nation to mobilize in WW I

And so it goes.

Details: The capitol is visible from anywhere in Salem, 900 Court St. NW. Call (503) 986-1388 for tour information.

Columbus Day Storm

There are storms, and then there was the October 12, 1962, doozy that slammed into Oregon. Discussion of the Columbus Day storm casts a dark cloud of gloom mixed with awe over those who remember it. What began as tropical typhoon Freda worked up winds that turned inland, hitting Oregon with a historic wallop. Winds of 170 mph whipped through coastal Astoria, hit Corvallis at 125 mph and Salem at 90 mph, and devastated Portland with a velocity of 116 mph. Damage to the state was over $170 million, including the downing of 6 billion board feet of timber. Forty-eight people died in the storm, twenty-four in Oregon.

ONLY ONE-SEVENTH OF OREGON'S temperate rain forests remain, making the 8,706 acres of Silver Falls State Park, Oregon's largest state park, a sanctuary. Located 26 miles from Salem, surrounded on three sides by farmland, and flanked on the east by the Cascade Range, this forest enshrouds you with the feeling of another world.

Within the park boundaries, 25 miles of trails meander through Douglas fir, hemlock, and cedar stands, then descend to a forest floor carpeted with ferns, mosses, and wildflowers, passing by or behind ten waterfalls on the way. Cupped in nature's amphitheater, the mist touches you both physically and emotionally. This park is another Oregon treasure. It wasn't always that way.

Much of what is now state park property had been logged, but locals still explored, camped, and picnicked in the extraordinary world around the creeks and falls—while others were looking to make a buck. In the late 1920s, D. E. Geiser, who owned the spectacular 177-foot South Falls, charged a dime admission to view the falls and a quarter to witness one of his stunts, which included pushing old cars off the falls. Another property owner ran a honky-tonk along the park's border; still another "entrepreneur" blared music that resonated through the canyon.

Beginning on March 21, 1931, under the guidance of Parks superintendent Samuel H. Boardman, the state began acquiring land in the Silver Falls area. One of the first purchases was Geiser's 100 acres, including South Falls: "This was the nest egg which hatched into a completed Silver Falls State Park," Boardman later wrote. Members of the Salem Chamber of Commerce became interested in the park project, and another 40 acres at North Falls was secured from the Silverton Lumber Company. The park was dedicated on July 23, 1933.

The federal government had acquired land adjoining the park deemed "sub marginal farm or over logged land" between 1934 and 1942, and in 1948 and 1949 it deeded nearly 6,000 acres, via the National Park Service, to the state of Oregon for recreational purposes. Land continued to be acquired, with the final inclusion in 1984, when Leo Cieslak bequeathed 160 acres, bringing the total acreage to 8,706, according to historian Lawrence Merriam.

While the Great Depression devastated much of the country, the development of Silver Falls' trails and buildings, along with forest restoration, resulted from President Franklin Roosevelt's Civilian Conservation Corps and Works Progress Administration. In 1935, CCC Camp State Park No. 9 opened, and 200 workers, along with WPA craftspeople and artisans, began a 7-year transformation of the park that visitors continue to enjoy today.

Details: Silver Falls State Park, off Oregon 214 near Sublimity, Oregon. A variety of accommodations, from campsites to ranch buildings to cabins and a conference center, are available. For information, visit www.oregonstateparks.org.

A Lodge and Its Furniture

The South Falls Lodge, built in 1940/41, reflects local workmanship and materials. Locally quarried hand-cut stone forms the foundation, and timber taken from within the park shapes the frame. Peeled logs and shingles give it its woodsy charm, and two massive interior fireplaces warm the interior.

One-of-a-kind myrtlewood furniture graces the interior of the rustic lodge and nearby Log Cabin. What were once two 5-foot-wide and 40-foot-long myrtlewood logs were transformed into twenty-five tables, eighty-two chairs, and eleven benches and a dining hutch. State Park superintendent Samuel Boardman had admired the furniture at Timberline Lodge on Mt. Hood, so he went to the source, Margery Hoffman Smith, director of Oregon Art Project, who designed all of the furnishings at Timberline, another WPA project. She and her staff designed the furniture for the concession building, which in its early years was operated as a restaurant. It's not every day you can sit down and relax on a bit of history.

THE ONLY HOUSE DESIGNED FOR Oregon by architect Frank Lloyd Wright is sited in a grove of oak trees near the city of Silverton. The 2,100-square-foot Usonian-style home was built in 1964 for Conrad and

When Mrs. Gordon died in 1997, the home languished while property prices soared for the 22-acres surrounding it. The new owners requested a demolition permit to make room for a very different house—

Twenty-six miles away a major public garden was being carved out of the farmland near the city of Silverton. The visionaries behind the Oregon Garden decided the house was a welcome addition to their grand plan. The structure was dismantled and on March 9, 2001, the main section of the house began a three-day journey to its new home on a flatbed truck. As for the remaining structure, each piece was dismantled, numbered, wrapped, and trucked to the Oregon Garden. The only things lost in the move were the first-floor concrete block walls and floor. At the new site, the Gordon House was situated amidst the ancient oaks with the same northern exposure of its original location. The intact second floor was set on blocks while the first floor concrete was rebuilt and the rooms reconstructed. When the upper level was lowered into place, it fit within one-sixteenth of an inch. The original beams, fretwork, and other priceless details were reinstalled, and one year from the time the Gordon House left its original lot it was reopened—not as a home, but a museum to showcase Frank Lloyd Wright's work and the architectural design that integrated the building into the natural environment.

"An idea is salvation by imagination"
—Frank Lloyd Wright

Evelyn Gordon. Wood, masonry, and glass create a contemporary haven of varied levels, where light plays off each surface as the day progresses. Yet Wright's Oregon legacy was slated for demolition, the compact gem to be replaced by a much larger trophy home.

not the middle-class model Wright began designing in the 1930s. Instead of being razed, the Gordon House was donated to the Frank Lloyd Wright Conservancy with the owner's stipulation that the home be moved off the Wilsonville property in 105 days.

Details: The Oregon Garden covers 70 acres and features seventeen specialty gardens. Within the grounds are an amphitheater, children's garden, agricultural market, education pavilion, and the Gordon House. Phone the gardens at (503) 874-8100 or (877) 674-2733; www.oregongarden.org.

WHAT THE BURGUNDY REGION IS TO France, the Dundee Hills are to Oregon. Not until 1966, when David Lette of the Eyrie Vineyards decided to plant Dijon clones of pinot noir and pinot gris vines on the rolling red hills of Dundee in Yamhill County, had anyone successfully raised the variety outside of Burgundy, France. Time was when Dundee was the Prune Capital of Oregon. Today, it is part of Oregon's best known and largest wine producing region, the north Willamette Valley. Here, in interlocking fertile slopes, tucked between the Pacific Ocean and the Cascade Range, are 70 percent of the state's 250 wineries.

The wine world took note in 1979 when Eyrie Vineyard's 1975 South Block Reserve pinot noir placed among the top ten in that category in a grand tasting competition in Paris. A similar competition was restaged in 1980, and Eyrie Vineyard's pinot noir placed second. Since then, Oregon vineyards and the wines they produce have steadily matured, garnering worldwide recognition and the kind of agricultural panache you just can't get from producing prunes.

Forty wine varietals are produced in the state, but Oregon's favorite grape is the temperamental and luscious red pinot noir, whose vines cover 6,450 acres and produce the state's flagship wine. The most widely raised white grape, pinot gris, fills 1,526 acres of sloping hills that capture a combination of occasional marine breezes, long hours of warm summer sunshine, and cool falls.

There are six official viticulture areas (appellations) in Oregon, where 100 percent of the grapes must be from the stated region to be used on the bottle label: the Willamette Valley, Umpqua Valley, Rogue Valley, Applegate Valley, Columbia Valley, and Walla Walla Valley. The latter two areas include vineyards in Washington and Oregon, but no Oregon wineries. In 2002, 1,073,177 cases of Oregon wine were bottled, creating $200 million in sales.

Although Willamette Valley wine pioneers such as David and Diane Lette (Eyrie Vineyards), Dick Erath (Erath Vineyard), and Bill Fuller (Tualatin Estates), to name a few, have made historic contributions to Oregon's wine industry, the first vineyards of what is considered contemporary Oregon wine were planted by Richard Somer, at Hillcrest Vineyards near Roseburg.

The charm of Oregon vineyards and wineries is often found not in grand chateaus but in their simple agriculture-based roots. With few exceptions, Oregon's winery facilities aren't the imposing architectural landmarks of California's Napa Valley but functional facilities where serious wine making takes place.

> **Details:** Wine and winery tour information can be found at www.oregonwines.org or by ordering the Oregon Winery Guide from the Oregon Wine Board, (503) 228-8336, or e-mail wineinfo@oregonwine.org.

Portland and the Gorge

Oregon's largest metropolitan area remains a place full of small towns. Each neighborhood offers its own sense of place, but Portland's heart is along the Willamette River where bridges link more than physical access. It's not surprising that Portland is home to the country's largest urban forest park, world's biggest used and new bookstore, and urbane architecture. A river town with a twist.

East of the city winds the breathtaking Columbia River Gorge, a thoroughfare for Native Americans, European explorers, and pioneers. Today, motorists and bicyclists can follow Interstate 84 or downshift to travel along portions of the restored Columbia River Highway and witness the spectacle of it all.

1 Oregon Convention Center, Multnomah Bridges, Portland Memorial Mausoleum, Portlandia, Powell's Books, Made in Oregon, Forest Park, Harvey Marine
2 Historic Columbia River Highway
3 McMenamins Edgefield
4 Crown Point
5 Multnomah Falls Lodge
6 Bonneville Dam
7 Mosier Twin Tunnels
8 Celilo Park
9 Timberline Lodge and Silcox Hut

Crown Point, Columbia River Gorge

WHAT BETTER WAY TO DIRECT VISITORS to a convention center than to create a landmark that reaches into the sky? In September 1991, the Oregon Convention Center opened in Portland. Phase I of the then 490,00-square-foot, $65 million facility's crowning glory was two 260-foot tinted green glass and steel towers resembling a pair of translucent Douglas fir trees. The convention center, designed by the architectural firm of Zimmer Gunsul Frasca (ZGF) Partnership, bucked the trend of impersonal voluminous spaces where conventioneers are warehoused to hawk and purchase goods. The 17-acre center site is replete with a park and public art with a regional spirit set amidst an innovative design. And the towers, instead of space for more convention hoopla and paraphernalia, serve a higher calling: two beautiful beacons in Portland's skyline. Their presence serves as guiding lights across the Willamette, an invitation to come see more of what Oregon has to offer.

During the planning and design process, the Center's location challenged the designers to give the facility a solid "come hither" element. The city and tri-county selected the convention site on the east side of the Willamette River, and ZGF's design principal, Robert J. Frasca, knew the complex needed a visual connection between the east and west sides of the city. "It was important that the convention center—because it was not in downtown—have a visual center," explained Mr. Frasca. So, he "invented these towers." Not only do the green spires connect the building to the city by adding an architecturally sophisticated element of eye candy to Portland's skyline, but the towers go beyond esthetics by creating a conduit of light into the con-

vention center. Conventioneers can enjoy the effects of the gigantic atrium design from the fourth-level Skyview Terrace restaurant, and the infusion of natural light is repeated by the use of pyramidal skylights throughout the convention center.

The spires' symbolism runs deep. The double towers echo the 1912 Steel Bridge towers that once dominated the city's skyline, and to Mr. Frasca the glass is the liquid color of water. "Oregon is famous for its water. [The towers] symbolized, not only the trees, but also the color of water and embracing the climate that I happen to love."

The Oregon Convention Center garnered ZGF Partnership the prestigious American Institute of Architects 1991 Firm Award. In

making the selection, "The AIA jury turned away from the East Coast establishment to honor a West Coast practice that offers architects across the country valuable lessons in urban and regional design." Construction of the convention center's

$116 million expansion began in 2001 and was completed in March 2003, doubling the size and making it the largest meeting facility in the Pacific Northwest.

Details: Oregon Convention Center, 777 NE. Martin Luther King Jr. Blvd., Portland, accessible via Interstate 5 North, Exit 302A (Rose Quarter), and Interstate 84 West, Exit 1 (Lloyd Blvd). MAX Light Rail stops 162 times a day at the Center, which is open to the public. Visit www.oregoncc.org.

ACTUALLY, WE'LL JUST STICK TO THE Portland metropolitan area, a city between two great rivers, the Willamette and the Columbia. The eight bridges that define Portland span the Willamette River. Driving in Portland, known for its pedestrian and bicycle-friendly layout and top-notch public transportation system, can be a challenge for us in cars. Getting lost means you drive over a bridge. To get back where you began means you drive over another bridge. I have traversed the Willamette dozens of times just to get to one place, so I have experienced Portland's bridges, perhaps not appreciating their history and engineering.

Let's begin with the newest and probably best known, the Fremont Bridge. Completed in 1973, the 1,255-foot Fremont Bridge is America's longest tied-arch bridge and one of only eighty steel tied-arch bridges in the United States. With two decks, one for westbound and the other for eastbound

traffic, it combines the grace of arches with high-tech engineering. Perhaps some of the Fremont's elegance can be attributed to input by the Portland Art Commission on its design. Although it's the newest Portland bridge, the name is for one of

Fremont Bridge

Oregon's early explorers, Capt. John Charles Fremont, whose surveys for the Oregon Trail and glowing reports became the fodder of many a pioneer's dream.

Hawthorne Bridge, constructed in 1910, stands as the oldest vertical-lift bridge in the world—and the oldest of Portland's river spans. Designed by John Alexander Low Waddell, the bridge was named after Dr. J. C. Hawthorne, one of the founders of the Oregon Hospital for the Insane. The bridge's original wooden decks were replaced with an open steel grated roadway in 1945, and the bridge was closed for a year of renovation in 1998. A favorite of pedestrians and bicyclists, the span is only 45 feet above the river.

In 1912, the city fathers decided that they wanted substantial bridges to take the city into its future. John Lyle Harrington and J. A. L. Waddell designed the Steel Bridge, which features two independent, movable decks. With proper maintenance, including lube jobs, Mr. Harrington claimed that his bridges would be permanent. The changing needs of Portland traffic have been met by the Steel Bridge: freight trains run

Hawthorne Bridge

Steel Bridge

Broadway Bridge

on the lower deck, automobiles and MAX light rail on the upper deck; there is a pedestrian and bicycle crossing on the lower deck. The control house atop the middle upper-level span adds to the immense bulk of the Steel Bridge.

Broadway Bridge, built in 1912/13, looks like something made from a gigantic erector set, but the complexities give it the distinction of being the world's largest Rall-type bridge (a Rall is the rolling mechanism that lifts a drawbridge). The Broadway's center span was built 90 feet above the water so that only the tallest of masted ships would require its opening, meaning fewer delays and cost to commuters and the city. Bicycle access was added in 1982.

Burnside Bridge, built in 1926, was one of the city's three major bridge projects during the frenzy of the 1920s. The double-leaf bascule draw-span (a bascule is a see-saw mechanism by which the roadway can "tilt up" for river traffic) replaced an earlier swing-span bridge. Walking across the Burnside is one of Portland's great pleasures. Foot travel gives you a chance to check out the decorative metal railings and Art Deco–inspired operator's housings with

Mediterranean tile roofs, the Made in Oregon sign (see p. 40), and the Old Town water tower. And if you think all bridges are made of steel and concrete, think again. According to author Sharon Wood Wortman, the Burnside piers are made of clusters of 40-foot-tall Douglas fir tree trunks, and each bascule pier is supported by 380 trees.

Portland's only suspension bridge, St. Johns, was dedicated during the Rose Festival of 1931. When it opened it was the longest rope-strand suspension bridge in the world, with a main span of 1,207 feet. Accommodating four lanes of traffic and two sidewalks, St. Johns is regarded as the aquatic gateway to the city. As such, it is appropriately designated a Portland Historical Landmark and eligible for placement on the National Register of Historic Places. The bridge engineer, David B. Steinman, believed that bridges should be both functional and beautiful. This bridge stands on Gothic shaped piers and is high enough for tall ships to pass under without disturbing its beauty.

The Morrison Bridge of today replaced the 50-year-old relic in 1958. The steel double-leaf Chicago-style fixed trunnion bas-

cule drawbridge sits on concrete and steel pilings. The main span is 284 feet long and 69 feet from the water. Designed by a Missouri and Portland firm, it is in the process of being retrofitted for earthquakes.

If St. Johns is the city's loveliest bridge, Marquam Bridge, constructed in 1966, is its ugly stepsister. Called a "freeway" bridge, the double-deck steel span was built on the cheap as the workhorse thoroughfare for traffic on Interstate 5 over the river to Portland. Although it is the busiest of the bridges, the thought of another dull-looking bridge prompted the design process that resulted in the Fremont Bridge almost a decade later.

That doesn't cover all the bridges of Multnomah County, or of Portland. If you're aching for more bridge information, check out *The Portland Bridge Book* by Sharon Wood Wortman. You won't be disappointed.

Details: If you arrived by boat from the west, you would encounter St. Johns, Fremont, Broadway, Steel, Burnside, Morrison, Hawthorne, and Marquam bridges in that order.

Burnside Bridge   **St. Johns Bridge**   **Morrison Bridge**

TIME WAS WHEN THE 48- BY 46-FOOT illuminated Made in Oregon sign on the north end of the Burnside Bridge, now with a leaping stag, advertised White Satin Sugar. Constructed in 1940 by Ramsay Signs, its original claim to signage fame was its shape—the state of Oregon. In 1950, according to Darryl Paulsen, president of Ramsay Signs, animation was added, and sugar seemed to pour into the White Satin bag.

Willamette Tent and Awning occupied the historic 1907 building underneath the sign in what is now called Old Town. The company evolved from tents to women's sportswear, and in 1957 Ramsay Signs transformed the White Satin sign into White Stag by changing "Satin" to "Stag" and adding the company's stag logo for the sign's lessee. Elizabeth Hirsch, wife of the building's owner, thought the stag would look splendid with a red nose, and it was added for the 1959 holiday season. A Portland landmark was in the making.

That official status transpired after the city's Historic Landmarks Commission nominated it and Gov. Neil Goldschmidt signed the declaration on February 27, 1978. By then, White Stag had moved its operation to Van Nuys, California, and the Made in Oregon Company occupied the building. Ramsay Signs took a leap of faith and continued to maintain and pay for the sign's upkeep after White Stag discontinued payments in 1988. "It's part of our heritage," explained Mr. Paulsen. "We were looking for a sponsor, but could never get anything finalized"—until Sam Naito, president of Made in Oregon, decided it was a natural for his company. The stag remained, and Ramsay Signs retooled the words to read "Made in Oregon" at a cost of $170,000 to the new lessee.

The sign stands out for a variety of reasons, not the least of which is the Portland sign ordinance that prohibits lighted signs facing the river. A variance kept the Portland beacon shining. "It's very unusual; everybody is happy, especially when we light the nose at Thanksgiving," said Mr. Naito.

Details: The Made in Oregon sign sits atop the 1907 White Stag (Hirsch-Weiss) building, 67 W. Burnside St. on the north end of the Burnside Bridge.

PORTLAND HOLDS THE DISTINCTIONS of having America's largest forested park in an urban city and of having the smallest park in the world. One reflects the local geology and the foresight of some of the region's population, the other the quirky self-deprecating humor that says something about this city.

For a town that went by the name "stump town," the 5,000-acre, 8-mile long swath of wilderness preserve along the Willamette River defies the old moniker. Forest Park is the ultimate "greenbelt." The land didn't begin with preservation in mind; in the 1800s a thick stretch of Douglas fir, hemlock, and Sitka spruce was something to log or clear for development. Once white settlers took over the land from the Indians, the new squatters were given parcels of the uplands along the northeast slope of the Tualatin Mountains in the Donation Land Claims of 1851. Try as they might, the land was too unstable to develop, and little by little parcels were donated to the city or claims defaulted.

A 30-acre parcel, now Macleay Park, was donated as a park in 1897, and two years later the Portland Municipal Park Commission was formed with Rev. Thomas Eliot as its most ardent board member. What the board did was, to say the least, progressive. In 1903 they hired the most prestigious landscape firm in the country, the Olmsted Brothers (Frederick Olmsted Sr. designed New York City's Central Park), to create Portland's master park plan. As for the forested mountain slope, John Olmsted saw no better use for it than a forested park: "It is true that some people look upon such woods merely as a troublesome encumbrance standing in the way of more profitable use of the land, but future generations will not feel so and will bless the men who were wise

enough to get such wood preserved." That said, the idea languished for four decades, while roads, landslides, timber cutting, wildfires, and unsuccessful oil drilling slowly altered the landscape. Finally, in 1948, the park was dedicated; when it came to naming the reserve, well, the city fathers went with the obvious: Forest Park.

The 30-mile-long Wildwood Trail traverses the park and is among 70 miles of interconnecting trails. The wooded park is home to more than one hundred bird and sixty mammal species. Then there are the trees: native evergreens, much of them logged, no longer dominate the forest, but the six conifer species along with fifteen hardwood varieties including red alder and big leaf maple offer a beautiful backdrop to the shrubs, vines, ferns, horsetails, and wildflowers that blanket Forest Park.

There's only one tree at Mill Ends Park—and it's tiny. Dropped in the middle of Southwest Naito Parkway and Taylor Street, at 452 square inches Mill Ends is smaller than most traffic medians. This is not a place to lounge around and have your lunch, and walking would mean one tight circle. It was journalist Dick Fagan who decided that a hole in the ground at the intersection beneath his *Oregon Journal* office needed some work. So he planted flowers, named the park after his column, "Mill Ends," and one thing led to another—including installation of a miniature Ferris wheel and bagpipe concerts; you get the idea.

1948 was a banner year for Portland parks. Not only was Forest Park dedicated, but also on St. Patrick's Day of that year Dick Fagan decided to dedicate tiny Mill Ends Park as part of Portland's parkscape. (In 1976, Portland officially did the same.) The Friends of Dick Fagan and the True

Believers in Patrick O'Toole (that would be the head leprechaun who lives on the patch) care for the park. Friends of Forest Park do the same thing on a rather larger scale. Both parks are under the management of Portland Parks and Recreation.

Details: Five parks are within Forest Park: Adams, Clark/Wilson, Holman, Macleay, and Pittock Acres. The Hoyt Arboretum, Japanese Gardens, and Washington Park and Portland Zoo are all adjacent to Forest Park. St. Helens Rd. and Skyline Blvd. run parallel to each edge of the park. Mill Ends Park is at the intersection of SW. Naito Parkway (Front Ave.) and Taylor St.

IF YOU'VE HEARD OF THE STATUE OF Liberty, you should have heard of Portlandia. No? Well, she is the symbol of Portland and the second-largest hammered copper statue in America right behind Ms. Liberty. Sculptor Raymond Kaskey took the image of a woman greeting traders to the city from Portland's city seal. What resulted is a flowing 36-foot-high picture of grace and strength. With her trident in hand,

Portlandia kneels down and reaches her hand out to the city.

While the city seal image of Lady Commerce depicts a wilderness scene in the background with mountains, forest, and sea, Portlandia is perched on a pedestal above the 5th Avenue entrance to the Portland Building. Architect Michael Graves designed Portland's first postmodern building and thought it needed a statue to finish off his creation. A competition followed, and Kaskey won the commission. Three years later, the lovely lady was on her way to Portland. Since Portlandia is one-third the size of the Statue of Liberty, she was sent in eight sections and assembled in a Portland shipyard. The controversial Portland Building wasn't embraced by all city residents, but Portlandia's entrance into the city was a popular and grand affair. She rode by river barge and truck to the downtown location with Portland residents cheering her on along the route. The new symbol of the city was dedicated on October 8, 1985.

Unlike her more famous New York City counterpart, there are no keychains, refrigerator magnets, or other kitsch to cheapen Portlandia's reputation. Mr. Kaskey retained full rights to the image. Still, in the spring of 2003, artist Amos

Latteier decided to have some fun with the sculpted figure, with the idea that folks could "Be Portlandia." Mr. Latteier set up a temporary installation, funded by the Regional Arts and Cultural Council, with hopes of getting more people up close and personal with Portland's art. Here individuals could pose as Portlandia in front of a backdrop (trident in hand), say cheese, and have their picture taken for posterity or their own personal oddball collection.

> **Details:** Portland Building, 1150 SW. 5th Ave. between Main and Madison.

Portlandia Poem

Poem at the base of the statue by Ronald Talney.

She kneels down
and from the quietness
of copper
reaches out.
We take that stillness
into ourselves
and somewhere
deep in the earth
our breath
becomes her city.
If she could speak
this is what
she would say:
Follow that breath.
Home is the journey we make.
This is how the world
knows where we are.

ANCHORED ON A FULL CITY BLOCK with gentrification closing in on its flanks, Powell's City of Books' entrance on West Burnside could be confused with a mission for the down-and-out. But inside, instead of handing out soup to the hungry, Powell's feeds hungry souls with such a smorgasbord of used and new books that you need a map to find your way around. Yet being lost in Powell's is part of its joy. Invariably, that's when you stumble upon some obscure, out-of-print title you have longed for or remembered you longed for or pretended you remembered you longed for. Whatever, if it's a book, it's either at Powell's or they can locate it for you. Not only do you find copies of the same title both used and new in hardback and paperback on the same shelf, but also they're at different price points depending on the edition and condition of each book. Two-thirds of the stock is used, out-of-print, or rare. The book inventory hovers at a million volumes in the Burnside store, making Powell's the largest used and new bookstore in the world. For many of the Northwest's bibliophiles, a trip to Powell's is a religious experience.

But the storyline of Powell's didn't begin in Portland, rather in Chicago where Michael Powell borrowed $3,000 and, while still doing graduate work at the University of Chicago, opened a bookstore. The store was an immediate success. Michael's father Walter, a retired Portland painting contractor, worked for his son for a summer, went home and began buying used books, and opened Powell's in Portland. Father and son joined forces and book sense, and in 1979 Powell's City of Books was born. Michael Powell purchased the business from his father in 1981. The Burnside store is the pilgrimage point for book lovers, but

there are four other full-service and three specialty Powell's stores in the Portland area, along with Powells.com on the web.

In addition to the book selection, Powell's City of Books is packed with authors who give readings or book signings or just shop for more books. It's an incestuous place. Some special features include the 4,700 topic sections, the Rare Books Room,

a Books Pillar holding up the porch at the NW. 11th and Couch entrance (complete the interred ashes of a diehard Powell's fan), the World Cup Café, and...the parking garage.

You'd think the plethora of books, the authors, the café would be enough, but you must experience the parking garage to get the full impact of Powell's City of Books. You don't have a car? This is the one time while you are in the City of Roses that you will regret not arriving on four wheels. With a 7-foot clearance and a steep one-way ramp, it's like driving into some twisted Chuck Palahniuk storyline. You can't figure out just where you're headed.

> **Details:** Powell's City of Books, 1005 W. Burnside St., (503) 228-4651, is open seven days a week, 365 days a year. Or visit www.powells.com.

AVAILABLE: INDIVIDUAL PERPETUAL-care home on four-acre, two-city block, eight-story Sellwood District property. Includes seven miles of marble hallways, statuary (two replicas of Michelangelo's Pieta, sculpted of marble from the same quarry as the original), Tiffany stained glass, brass and bronze detailing, spiral stairways, fountains, elevators and quiet neighbors. Overlooks Oaks Bottom Wildlife Refuge and amusement park.

Founded in 1901, the Portland Memorial Mausoleum and Funeral Home in southeast Portland houses the remains of some of the city's most noted individuals and their families. First designed as a crematorium and place to store ashes, it has expanded over the century into a full-service funeral home and mazelike mausoleum chock full of vault-lined columbariums, crypts, urns, and nooks within family "rooms" to sit and think about life.

The main offices and funeral home are housed in a Mediterranean-style building at SE. Bybee Boulevard and SE. 14th Avenue.

Behind that stand the early, architecturally significant structures and modern concrete additions that rise eight stories from the marshy and creepy Oaks Bottom swamp.

The Rose Chamber, the original building, is grouped with the Lily, Daisy, Tulip, Carnation, and other flower-inspired rooms one floor below. The entire mausoleum interconnects by vault-lined hallways, stairways, and elevators. Before you plunge in, note the Rae crypt in the courtyard, the largest family crypt in the compound, and the American carillon with seventy-five

miniature bronze bells in the meditation garden. Enter the mausoleum through the double doors next to the Rae crypt, and you'll be on the fifth floor where you'll find the Washington Corridor with its amazing display of stained glass at the end of individual alcoves with family members interred on each side. Various wings of the mausoleum are named after U.S. presidents, then morph into religious monikers.

With photocopies of all eight floors in my hand, I was lost within ten minutes. No wonder, with 98,000 residents and room for more, numerous viewing and meditation rooms, fountains, and domes, it is the largest mausoleum west of the Mississippi and has the distinction of being the first crematorium in the Northwest. When the business first opened, the Portland Railway serviced the facility complete with a funeral car with space for the grieving family and casket.

Walking through the mausoleum rates a ten on the strangeness scale, but it's worth it to take a deep—albeit damp and chilly—breath, slow down, and read the names chiseled on the vaults. Portland architect John Yeon and Humphrey Bogart's first wife, Mayo Methot, are among them. I began to wonder: Were all women born in the mid-1800s named Tillie, Ida, Clara, and Gertrude?

In addition to the history, the stained glass, two Pietàs and other statues, the six-story spiral marble staircase, and open five-story octagonal balconies with fountain at the foundation are worth seeking out.

Details: The Portland Memorial Mausoleum and Funeral Home, 6705 SE. 14th Ave., is open to the public. For hours, call (503) 236-4141.

THERE ARE HUNDREDS—PROBABLY thousands—of giant Paul Bunyans, Blue Oxen, Muffler Men service station icons, and other oversized roadside memorabilia, but in Portland (or Aloha, to be exact) there is Harvey Marine, a giant two-story rabbit. If you're driving down 185th Street, you can't miss him.

Harvey didn't start out as a rabbit. He originally was a giant gas station guy dropped off at Ed Harvey's Marine shop to have a little fiberglass repair work done after a storm blew him down. The work was completed, but no one came to get the big guy. Eventually, Ed decided to take put a rabbit's head on the gas station man's shoulders. The rest is roadside history.

The whole trend of creating oversized animals and people has some legitimate historic origins, according to Mirra Meyers of Oregon's State Historic Preservation Office. She says that most were created after World War II when service people returned from the trenches with a pent-up need to create things: anything, especially things that were big and silly. And it wasn't just in the United States; such images are all over the world.

Harvey's life as the beacon guarding the entrance to Harvey Marine has gone pretty smoothly. And Harvey has a wardrobe: come each holiday season he is decked out in appropriate wear. With the exception of an ear being ripped off by vandals and general maintenance by Ed Harvey, Harvey the Giant Rabbit's life has been full. And according to Ed, the rabbit's fame is growing: "He's on that Roadside America website, something in Texas, the chamber of commerce." You can't keep a giant rabbit down.

Details: Harvey Marine, 21250 SW. TV Highway, Aloha, (503) 649-5551.

Other Oddly Shaped Things

Sandy Jug Tavern: A tiny tavern the shape of a whiskey jug can be found at 7427 NE. Sandy Blvd.

Paul Bunyan: Yes, Portland has one, too! This 35-foot-high concrete statue was erected in 1959 to greet visitors to the Oregon Centennial Exposition. Paul, sans Babe, stands at the intersection of NE. Interstate Ave. and N. Denver Ave.

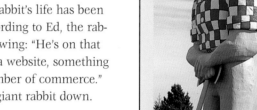

A&W Family: This transplanted family of four, once mascots of a now defunct A&W restaurant, found new life in Hillsboro. Mom, dad, and the kids—burgers and root beer in hand—are now planted in shrubbery between the tennis courts at the Hillsboro Aquatic Center, 953 SE. Maple. St.

JERRY GARCIA STANDS IN THE GARDEN, the former residents of the old Poor Farm still lurk in the hallways, lovers stroll through the grounds, beer flows at the brewery, wine ferments in the winery; there are vineyards, restaurants, movies, music, golf, and art. Yes, this 38-acre estate, once the County Poor

Farm, has found a brighter day. Reincarnated into McMenamins Edgefield in Troutdale, life on the farm is indeed good, very good.

The whimsical and ongoing transformation of the 1911 structure, outbuildings, and grounds is testimony that a couple of slightly off-center business visionaries, who opened the state's first brewpub, know what makes guests happy. That happiness is found sans guestroom televisions, telephones, and anything remotely stuffy. The Edgefield is the kind of place where you check your worries at the door, then step into Mike and Brian McMenamin's world. If you can't have fun here, you have a problem.

Built as a refuge for the down-on-their-luck folk of the county, an innovative program in social welfare, the Poor Farm fed, housed, and clothed those who could not do it for themselves. In exchange, those fit enough worked the fields, dairy, and hog farm. While the residents were predomi-

nately indigents, their digs were hardly the flophouse variety. The county prided itself in constructing an elegant red brick Georgian-style manor. When the main building and power station (now a pub and theater) were completed, 211 inmates moved in—75 of them bedridden. The Poor Farm population peaked during the Great Depression to over 600 inmates, and as social moirés changed, so did the facility. By 1964 the complex was renamed the Edgefield Center, now with its primary mission as that of a nursing home. In 1982 the last patient transferred from the nursing home, and the compound was put up for sale.

Naturally, there were those who thought demolition was a tidy solution, but the Troutdale Historical Society and Troutdale mayor Sam Cox saw things differently. Eventually others came to believe that the historic complex should not be destroyed but rather readapted to another use. Finding a buyer was another matter. In 1990 the dilapidated buildings were put on the National Register of Historic Places; that same year the McMenamins purchased for $500,000 what can only be described as one big challenge.

"When Mike and Brian first went to look at Edgefield, it was a wreck. But they saw past the tumbled down buildings, graffiti, vandalism, and toll the elements had taken on the property. They saw that this could be a village to expand upon their definition of what a good pub should be," explained Tim Hills, McMenamins' historian. "That 'pub' would include 38 acres and various buildings that would be filled with artists, brewers, dis-

tillers, chefs and families. They could see what it could be, but the bankers couldn't. It took several meetings with several loan officers to take that leap of faith with them."

Today, guests take their own leap into the Edgefield world, perhaps most visibly felt in the artwork. The Poor Farm history (and that of the region) is interpreted in every nook and cranny of the Edgefield. Two dozen artists, commissioned to transform the institutional 100-room main house into a work of art, created more whimsy than Disneyland—and with more soul.

Details: Edgefield is in Troutdale, twenty minutes from downtown Portland off Interstate 84, east to Exit 16, south on 238th Dr. to Halsey St., then east for a quarter of a mile. This is a perfect beginning or end to a trip along the Historic Columbia River Highway. Call (503) 669-8610, or see www.mcmenamins.com.

More Where That Came From

Edgefield was McMenamins first lodging venture, and McMenamins fans make pilgrimages to all of the historic hotels. Each facility is unique, but a common theme of unusual packages (Raft, Draft and Cast Wilderness tours), great music, movies, wine, beer, quality dining, and plenty of art exudes from each destination. While there are dozens of the brothers' brewpubs in Oregon and Washington, here are their historic Oregon hotels:

Kennedy School, Northeast Portland: A 1915 school where thousands of Portland children were educated now offers lodging in thirty-five guestrooms, restaurants, bars, brewery movies, a gym, and the usual frivolity. What isn't fun about staying in rooms each named after a teacher complete with chalkboards.

Grand Lodge, Forest Grove: When it opened in 1922, the lodge was the Masonic and Eastern Star Home, where members of the fraternal order spent their elder years. The 13-acre grounds are a smaller version of Edgefield with seventy-seven overnight rooms.

Hotel Oregon, McMinnville: The rejuvenated 1905 hotel in the heart of Oregon's wine country caters to wine tasting tours (or you can check out Howard Hugh's Spruce Goose at the Evergreen Aviation Museum), with forty-two rooms, restaurant, and, yes, artwork.

The White Eagle, Portland: Billed as rock n' roll lodging, the White Eagle serves up meals, drinks, and music in its main-level saloon, with overnight accommodations upstairs. This storied working class haunt with roots stretching back to 1905 is rife with lore and live music tradition. Music plays until 1 or 2 A.M., so if you stay overnight, it should be for the music.

IT'S SAID THAT OREGONIANS LIKE TO think of Timberline Lodge as their collective home. And what a home it is. Built during the Great Depression as part of the WPA projects, the lodge is the state's most meaningful and remarkable building. President Franklin Roosevelt dedicated Timberline in a live radio address on September 28, 1937. The architectural design was dubbed Cascadian after the range it stands on and reflects its proximity to the city of Portland and the magnitude of Mt. Hood, whose peak thrusts up behind. Everything in Timberline is hand-made, from the massive hand-hewn timbers to the wrought iron lamps, chandeliers, and andirons, loomed and woven fabrics and rugs, and custom-created furniture;

it is one gigantic piece of historic art. That piece of art is cared and tended for by the managers, RLK Company, who saved the lodge from ruin, the U.S. Forest Service, and the nonprofit Friends of Timberline.

Timberline does not stand alone. One thousand feet above the lodge, a mile above timberline at 7,000 feet elevation, stands a miniature version of the lodge. The exquisite stone and timber Silcox Hut was built in 1939 by the same laborers and craftspeople who created the lodge. Its was originally the upper terminus and warming station for the Magic Mile Chairlift, the second-oldest chairlift in the United States. It sheltered climbers and skiers for 25 years and then fell into disrepair. Vandals and the harsh

weather took their toll, and after shingles were torn off for firewood, windows broken, and graffiti marred the walls, it looked like demolition would be the hut's fate.

But in 1985, the hut was put on the National Register of Historic Places, and the Friends of Silcox Hut was established as a nonprofit group to restore the building. The restoration and adaptive reuse of the hut gar-nered numerous awards, including recognition by the American Institute of Architects.

Today the building is a sanctuary of sorts where climbers stop for hot cocoa or tea before their ascent of the state's most climbed (and treacherous) peak. Groups can rent the hut, settle in for unsurpassed stargazing, have dinner catered from Timberline's superb Cascade Dining Room, then bunk down in, well, bunks. During May, Silcox Hut can be rented by individuals on a first-come, first-served basis.

> **Details:** The exit to Timberline Lodge and Silcox Hut is on U.S. 26, 60 miles east of Portland. Call (800) 547-1406 for information, or visit www.timberlinelodge.com.

AT A TIME WHEN FREEWAY EXPANSION is the expected norm, when roads are wide, wider, widest, the two-lane Historic Columbia River Highway is an anomaly. Markers off Interstate 84 along the Columbia River Gorge direct motorists to sections of the restored highway, where they downshift and find themselves on a route so exquisitely executed that the road itself is a National Historic Landmark.

That construction was the vision of Sam Hill, an entrepreneur, lawyer, and advocate of road construction and improvement. He and engineer Samuel Lancaster, with the support of Portland civic leaders, determined that a road from Portland to The Dalles not only was needed and feasible but should be beautiful. Along the route of a highway was constructed with an eye to match the surrounding detail.

Multnomah County, and private interests came together, and in 1922 the first major paved road in the Pacific Northwest was completed. In addition to a two-lane road were elegant bridges, parapet-arched stone guardwalls, and tourist pullouts. Lancaster made sure that the road skirted or created access to many of the Gorge's scenic wonders and hiking trails. Italian masons and craftsmen were hired to build hand-cut stone steps and view structures. When the highway opened, the *Illustrated London News* called it the "King of the Roads." The name stuck.

Only 14 years after the highway's completion, many of those very wonders were lost with the construction of the Bonneville Dam. Then, in the 1950s and 1960s, the four-lane Interstate 84 paved over or bypassed stretches of the Historic Highway; tunnels were filled and the past seemed lost.

The new interstate highway expedited truck and motorist travel, but the leisurely pace of the trip was left to diehard road fans that stuck to the remaining portions of the old route. That route's masonry work, railings, and the road itself decayed over time. In 1981 the National Park Service put together a maintenance guide that included repairing rock walls, bridge railings, and other historic portions of the highway. The Oregon Department of Transportation (ODOT) undertook that work. Since then various projects have been implemented to repair and restore the existing historic highway, parking lots, and bridges. The government agencies that take or oversee these projects include the U.S. Forest Service, ODOT, Federal Highway Commission, and Oregon Parks and Recreation Department, along with numerous volunteer organizations, since

The tenants of organic architecture focus on the melding of a building with its setting. Here in the spectacular Columbia Gorge—with Northwest greenery dripping with atmosphere, waterfalls dropping off cliffs, rock formations formed 40 million years ago, and rich temperate rain forests banking every curve until the roadway climbs into the more arid eastern end—a Native American trade corridor, the Lewis and Clark expedition, and pioneers on the Oregon Trail would be a road for the up-and-coming automobile.

Timber entrepreneur Simon Benson donated $10,000 in 1912 for construction at Shellrock Mountain, and the following year road construction began in Multnomah County. The State Highway Department,

the highway travels through various public lands as well as private property.

In 1987, the Oregon Legislature created the Historic Columbia River Highway Advisory Committee to advise ODOT, Oregon Parks and Recreation, and the Federal Highways Commission regarding restoration work on the old highway. The Legislature decided that, although the destroyed portions of the Historic Highway had been lost to motorized travel, restoration as a hiking and biking trail was feasible. The reopening of the stretch of highway from Hood River to the Mosier section began in 1995. The project was tackled in six sections, with Phase I being the opening of the Mosier Twin Tunnels, which since the 1950s had been filled with rubble and closed to traffic. The ongoing restoration of this scenic slice of the Historic Columbia River Highway has earned awards including

the Federal Highway Administration 1997 Environmental Excellence Award for restoration of the Hood River to Mosier section and the Oregon Forest Highway Enhancement Program in 2003.

Today, the driving trip is a constant reminder of a time when life ran at a slower pace, and the hiking and biking trails offer rare opportunities to gaze out at the wonder of the Columbia River Gorge.

Details: The Historic Highway begins off Interstate 84 at Exit 18 near Troutdale and, going west, ends at Dodson/Ainsworth, Exit 35. Most of the highway was lost between Dodson/Ainsworth and Hood River, where it picks up again and continues until near The Dalles. A portion of the last leg is no longer drivable, but it has been restored to hiking and biking trails between Hood River and Mosier. From Mosier to The Dalles, the final motor traffic leg of the Historic Highway is intact.

Stops Along the Highway

Chanticleer Point: (photo p. 50) Leaving Portland, this is the first viewpoint where you can see the expanse of the river, highway, and the next vista point. It is also the site of the Portland Women's Forum State Park, named for the group that purchased and donated the 3.7 acres including the overlook to the state park system.

Crown Point and Vista House: Crown Point and its jewel, Vista House, are what you see looking east from Chanticleer Point. Vista House was inspired by German Art Nouveau architecture and designed by Edgar M. Lazarus; it is listed on the National Register of Historic Places. Crown Point is a National Natural Landmark. And, of course, the Historic Highway is a National Historic Landmark (only one of three such roadways in the country). Don't forget that the gorge itself is a National Scenic Area.

Falls and More Falls: Each waterfall is different from the last...they are clearly marked, but the most famous is Multnomah Falls and the 1925 Multnomah Falls Lodge (on the National Register of Historic Places) designed by noted Portland architect A. E. Doyle and constructed by the city of Portland. Simon Benson donated the land to the city of Portland. If the lot is full, pull into Wahkeena Falls. Whatever your fancy and ability, take a walk or hike along one of the falls trails.

Bridge of the Gods: Travelers can exit Interstate 84 at Exit 44 to cross the Bridge of the Gods, but if possible it is best to bike or hike along the trail between the Bonneville Dam and Cascade Locks along the route of the old highway to the 1926 Bridge of the Gods. This location was originally a natural "bridge" forming Cascade Rapids created by the A.D. 1260 Cascade landslide or by a violent conflict between three mountain deities—whichever you choose to believe.

Mosier Twin Tunnels: (photos p. 51 and above) Watchful motorists can catch a glimpse of the Mosier Twin Tunnels high on the cliffs above Interstate 84 at the Mosier exit. To experience the tunnels and roadway, take Exit 64 for the western trailhead or Exit 69 for the eastern trailhead. The twin tunnels link the wet western end of the Gorge to the dry eastern Columbia River plateau, and the cliff-hugging highway is a thrill.

Rowena Crest: Crown Point and Vista House get all the attention, but Rowena Crest Overlook and its spiraling looped ascent presents an unobstructed view up and down the Columbia River, including the 230-acre Tom McCall Preserve.

THE BONNEVILLE LOCK AND DAM'S construction was the first of eight federal locks and dams on the Columbia and Snake rivers that changed the face, economy, and environment of the Pacific Northwest. Built as part of the federal works projects during the Great Depression, Bonneville Dam was dedicated by President Franklin D. Roosevelt on September 28, 1937, when he proclaimed the dam would create "more wealth, better living and greater happiness to our children." What it immediately created in 1933 when construction began were jobs: 50 cents an hour for unskilled workers and $1.20 for skilled labor. When fully under way, the total workforce both on and off the site averaged

3,000 people. A work camp for 400 of those laborers was constructed near the site. All told, the construction cost of the first powerhouse, lock, and dam was $88.4 million.

Constructed and operated under the auspices of the U.S. Army Corps of Engineers, the Bonneville Lock and Dam was designed to generate cheap hydroelectric power and expedite ship navigation by creating a 48-mile-long reservoir behind the dam for vessels to navigate the Columbia River up to the Dalles more easily. Vessels passed through the 76-foot-wide and 500-foot-long historic lock from 1938 to 1994, when it was "mothballed." Also part of the design were fish ladders for adult migrating fish. Juvenile fish are diverted through a bypass system away from the powerhouse turbines.

The Bonneville Lock and Dam was placed on the National Register of Historic Places as a historic district in 1986. The 97-acre district includes seven parts: the Colonial Revival–style administration building and auditorium, spillway dam, powerhouse, navigation lock, fish hatchery, and landscaping. The facility operates a visitor center, park rangers give tours (not as extensive since the terrorist attacks of 9/11) of the powerhouse, and fish ladders can be viewed from an underwater level.

Dam Facts

Power from the Powerhouse: The ten-generator first powerhouse has a total generating capacity of 526,700 kilowatts.

Second Powerhouse: Between 1974 and 1981, a second powerhouse was constructed on the Washington side of the river. This eight-generator structure has a total generating capacity of 558,200 kilowatts.

Hydropower: What does that mean? Well, between the two powerhouses, over one million kilowatts is produced—enough to supply nearly 500,000 homes for a year.

Columbia River Basin: The Bonneville Dam, one of eight dams on the Lower Columbia and Snake rivers, is among more than 400 dams that block river flow in the Columbia Basin (from Lewiston, Idaho, to the Pacific),

making it the most hydroelectrically developed river system in the world. That power goes into a power grid system.

Who Gets the Power? Power is bought and sold within the Pacific Northwest, Canada, and California, making it an interregional and international network.

Large Lock: Bonneville's 1938 lock was the largest single-lift lock in the world, with a 60-foot vertical lift that could simultaneously hold two barges and a tugboat.

Larger Lock: The 1993, $341 million Bonneville lock can hold five barge tows and can move a vessel in thirty minutes what used to take several hours.

Employment: More than 100 workers staff the Bonneville Lock and Dam.

Counting Fish: One of those jobs includes counting the various species of adult fish moving up the fish ladder. The fish counters sit at a window counting and calibrating each fish from April 1 to October 31. The numbers are posted outside the counting room door. On September 25, 1903, the count was 6,746 chinook, 1,194 chinook jack, 1,649 coho, 112 jack coho, 1,660 steelhead, and 66 lamprey. During a heavy summer run, 80,000 fish are counted in a day. There are two fish counters per 8-hour shift, seven days a week.

Herman and the Hatchery: The Bonneville Fish Hatchery includes ponds for fingerling smolts and outdoor feeding tanks where you can toss fish food (25 cents a handful) to the sturgeon and steelhead. Then head to the viewing room below and take a look at Herman the monster sturgeon. One big fish.

THE FLOODING OF THE ANCIENT

Celilo Falls fishing grounds on the Columbia River east of The Dalles is one of Oregon's saddest stories—the kind of devastating step one culture takes that destroys another. So, what was once a stunning 20-foot falls cut through the basalt of the Columbia River Gorge and ancient fishing grounds is now a park full of interpretive signs attempting to explain what was there and what was lost.

The massive falls were native peoples' fishing grounds thousands of years before the Lewis and Clark's Corps of Discovery, the hunters, trappers, miners, slave traders, or pioneers ever set their sights on the great Columbia River. Although whites were impressed with Indians fishing techniques (they taught the Corps new methods of catching and preserving salmon), most failed to understand the cultural meaning of salmon to the native peoples.

White settlement and reservations officially displaced native peoples beginning with the Treaty of 1855. These treaties did include tribal rights "of taking fish in all streams, where running through or bordering said

reservation." By the 1920s, Indians from the Yakama, Warm Springs, and Umatilla reservations and nontribal residents of Celilo Village formed the Celilo Fish Committee to defend their rights. Those fishing rights were broken with the flooding from each dam. The construction of the Bonneville Dam in 1938 alone inundated thirty-five native fishing sites. and in-lieu sites were slow in coming if they came at all.

But the date that marks the real breaching of both the river and the cultures was March 10, 1957, when The Dalles Dam stopped the downstream surge of the Columbia River. Six hours later, Celilo Falls was under water.

Where hundreds fishing scaffolds once clung to the cliffs bordering the falls, where trading, feast, and religious ceremonies were once held, there was now a blanket of water. The government paid for flooding the fishing sites, but the dam destroyed a cultural and economic cornerstone of Indian life. What the government did not buy were the fishing rights of the tribes. After the destruction of Celilo Falls, the government created a 300-acre reservation that includes the Celilo Indian Village and fishing grounds. In a landmark 1974 court decision, the Treaty of 1855 interpretation entitled tribes to catch up to 50 percent of the harvestable fish.

At the end of Celilo Park along the Columbia is a fenced parking lot where salmon are hauled in by tribal members. Dozens of huge tubs of shimmering silver salmon, netted the previous night, were being cleaned and weighed the day I was there. Celilo Park is filled with interpretive signs about the flooding of Celilo (Wyam) Falls, and at certain times of year visitors can see tribe members' nets laid across the river. The most interesting of the interpretive signs ends with the sentence "The loss of Wyam Falls did not mean the loss of the Indian way of life." In neat black ink, the word "not" has been crossed out.

A long-planned renovation of Celilo Village with new homes, roads, water, and sewer began at press time.

Details: Celilo Park on Celilo Lake is operated by the U.S. Army Corps of Engineers. Take Exit 97 off Interstate 84 about 12 miles east of The Dalles. A traditional longhouse stands in Celilo Indian Village on the opposite side of the freeway. The falls were 8 miles east of the The Dalles Dam.

Eastern Oregon

Wallowa Mountains, near Halfway

The Oregon Trail has left more than wagon train tracks in eastern Oregon's landscape. Today, long, lonely stretches over a network of two-lane roads offer travelers insight into a history that lives on. While the pioneer past leaves visitors in awe, the prehistoric, geologic, and Native American stories are sagas of their own. Here visitors must take time to savor the solitude in a place so full of rough and tumble revelations they will leave with an instant longing to return to a place where Chief Joseph made a stand, Basque sheepherders carved out a culture, and miners and ranchers battled the elements.

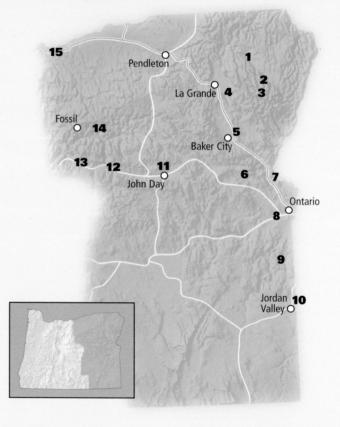

1	Wallowa County	**9**	Leslie Gulch and Lake Owyhee
2	Chief Joseph Monument	**10**	Basque Fronton Court
3	Eagle Gap Wilderness	**11**	Kam Wah Chung
4	Hot Lake Mineral Springs Resort	**12**	Upper John Day River Overlook
5	Oregon Trail Interpretive Center	**13**	Henry the Bear
6	Malheur Cemetery	**14**	Kinzua Hills Golf Club
7	Farewell Bend	**15**	Deschutes Crossing
8	Vale Murals		

TWO STONE GATEPOSTS BUILT BY THE Umatilla Tribal Civilian Conservation Corps in 1938–40 mark the entrance to Old Chief Joseph's gravesite. The 5.1-acre cemetery is a national historic park in memory of Chief Joseph, who died in 1871. The elder leader of the Nez Perce Tribe, Chief Joseph supported the tribe's longstanding peace with whites. His support was rewarded with deceit when almost 6 million acres of land decreed as part of the Nez Perce reservation was taken back by the U.S. government in 1863. Old Chief Joseph, outraged by the betrayal, denounced the government and the Bible (he had converted to Christianity) and refused to move his band from the Wallowa Valley or sign a treaty for the shrunken reservation boundaries. His dying words to his son, Chief Joseph, were: "My son, my body is returning to my mother earth, and my spirit is going very soon to see the Great Spirit Chief. When I am gone, think of your country. You are the chief of these people. They look to you to guide them. Always remember that your father never sold his country. You must stop your ears when ever you are asked to sign a treaty selling your home. My son, never forget my dying words. This country holds your father's body. Never sell the bones of your father and your mother."

The stone monument is a sacred place to the Nez Perce, and a small reminder of the saga that transpired. The Nez Perce retreat, 2,000 miles toward Canada, where the Indians thought Canadians respected treaties, began here. It did not end in Canada, rather 30 miles from the border where what remained of the 300 Nez Perce, including Chief Joseph, surrendered. Instead of being sent to the Lapwai Reservation in Idaho, they were herded to

Oklahoma. Finally, Chief Joseph returned to the northwest at Colville Reservation in Washington, where he was buried.

The traditional stone monument to his father, built in 1926 when the chief's grave was moved, is set on a rise above Wallowa Lake. It is the kind of monument constructed in Christian cemeteries. But it is the scrubby bush next to the monument, strewn with beads, dream weavers, and trinkets, and the base of the monument, where spools of thread, bundles of sage, long braids, and stones are placed, that

illustrate the difference between traditional grave markers and contemporary tokens of remembrance.

Details: Old Chief Joseph Monument is a mile south of Joseph on Oregon 82. This is one of four Oregon sites among the thirty-eight sites of Nez Perce National Historical Park scattered across the states of Idaho, Oregon, Washington, and Montana. The Wallowa Lake monument signals the beginning of the Nez Perce Trail, which stretches to Bear Paw Battlefield near Chinook, Montana.

THE SMALL TOWNS AND ROLLING LAND-scape of Wallowa County are gems, and worth more than a "drive through" on Highway 82.

For years **Joseph,** population just over 1,000, was best known for its location near the Wallowa Lake and Mountains, its Wild West history, and Chief Joseph, the Nez Perce leader who claimed the valley as his tribe's ancestral home. A post office was established in 1880, and the town was incorporated in 1887. Then in the 1940s,

7235, if you're interested in foundry tours.

If you're interested in more that art, stop by the Wallowa County Museum, 110 S. Main Street. The museum building housed the First Bank of Joseph when it was built in 1888; it was entered on the National Register of Historic Places in 1978. Most of the historic buildings on Main Street are brick, since the city had its own brickyard and kiln.

We pulled into **Enterprise** and immediately noticed the distinctive stone buildings.

The 1909 Wallowa County Courthouse; the 1899 E. R. Bowlby Building, 110 W. Main Street; the 1918 Burnaugh Building—cut stone buildings everywhere! Charlotte McIver, Wallowa County Clerk, filled us in. The stone came from a quarry on the ranch of Enoch Bowlby, an early homesteader. Since a few stonemasons had settled in the area, they were able to cut and shape the stone that was then hauled by six-horse teams and sold for a dollar per cord.

the sign at the north end of town became its signature: "This little town is HEAVEN to us, Don't drive like HELL through it."

Today Joseph is a mecca for bronze artwork and a tourist destination. There are seven bronze sculptures along Joseph's Art Walk. All of that bronze is locally produced at not one but three bronze foundries. Take a look at the bronze on the Art Walk, then call Valley Bronze, (541) 432-7445; Parks Bronze, (541) 426-495; or Manuel Museum, (541) 431-

If Joseph is too artsy and Enterprise too big, head to **Lostine,** where grazing horses munch on the grass of Ollis Sports Field. This is the smallest town in Wallowa County. Many of the original buildings were lost in a fire in 1893, but others were built. The charm of the place is that it is neither decaying nor overrun by "renewal." And not everything is small: the town's biggest undertaking was the 1902 construction of a $6,000 school house. It still stands,

in no small part because it is built of the same sort of stone found in Enterprise, but this time donated by G. W. Cray's quarry on the Wallowa River. The two-story school was used into the 1960s as a public school but was closed after a district consolidation.

For years the school structure warehoused tires. In 2001, the solid stone school opened with a different calling as the Providence Academy of Classical Christian Education (above). Headmaster Archie Buck is rightly proud of the restoration of the school, now

full of students instead of tires. "Imagine, studded tires rolled down this hall," he explained of the refinished hardwood floors.

If Lostine got its name from an Illinois or Kansas town (depends who you ask), it had to be because of the farmland. The historic barns that dot the landscape make for a Grandma Moses setting. The barns are so lovely that Enterprise Hometown Improvement Group put together two self-guided, self-drive tours of sixteen **Wallowa County historic barns;** among them are an octagonal barn in Joseph, the 1898 Wade house and barn, and the Eggleson barn (below), possibly the most photographed barn in the region. Working barns are becoming a thing of the past, so this collection makes for a wonderful side trip. The color tour booklets with pictures and historic information on barns can be purchased at The Bookloft in Enterprise, Book Corner in Joseph, or Wallowa County Chamber of Commerce; sponsored by the Enterprise Hometown Improvement Group. (541) 426-0219.

End of the Road

Wallowa Lake Lodge: At the end of 1,506-acre Wallowa Lake at the base of the Wallowa Mountains is this 1920s lodge. No telephones, no television, lovely guestrooms, lush lawn, big porch with lake view. Don't miss it. Details at www.wallowalake.com, (541) 432-9821.

Eagle Cap Wilderness: This 356,461-acre wilderness, part of the Wallowa-Whitman National Forest, holds the eight peaks of the Wallowa Mountains. Established in 1940, the wilderness is full of high alpine lakes and meadows, granite peaks, glaciated valleys, and forests. Elevations range from 5,000 to 10,000 feet. Access if from Wallowa Lake, a mile away.

HEAT RISES FROM THE PAVEMENT ON State Highway 203 between La Grande and Union. It is August and the temperature holds steady in the high 90s. The idea of a mirage is not outlandish, so when the decaying red brick Hot Lake Mineral Springs Resort appears behind a veil of steam rising from a lily- and cattail-clogged lake, we pull over.

This National Historic Place illustrates how little respect is shown to some of our historic buildings: the tattered white balustrades hang from balconies barely supported by rotting columns that once outlined the first floor solarium; all of the windows are gone; half of the roof is missing; the grounds have long ago gone wild; and the octagonal spring house sits abandoned like a grounded ship by the lake. Barbed wire surrounds the property with "Open—No Trespassing" instructions oddly juxtaposed from the wire fencing. The words HOT LAKE perch precariously in huge gold letters on top of the old three-story building. More easily read is this sign: For Sale by Owner, 40-acre historic site.

Two-and-a-half million gallons of 185°F mineral water rises to the surface into Hot Lake each day, making it Oregon's largest hot spring. Long before the white man developed the springs and lake, native peoples used it as a sacred place. The first recorded owner of the Hot Lake property was William Clark, who sold it to Samuel Newhard in 1872. The resort of the 1880s was a frame hotel with a row of bathhouses. What jump-started the real estate development of the property was the addition of the railway line, which assured easy access for "patients" ready and willing to give the healing powers of the mineral steam and waters a shot at curing everything from eczema to rheumatism.

The company name and ownership changed and moved about, but the goal was usually the same: to turn this geothermally active spot into another Arkansas Hot Springs, drawing crowds to the hotel and sanatorium where guests received first-class medical treatment along with plenty of pampering and entertainment.

Yet Hot Lake was more than that. In 1908, a 65,000-square-foot, brick, U-shaped hospital was completed. At the height of its success in the 1920s, under the tutelage of Dr. William Phy, it was called the Mayo Clinic of the West. With four physicians, an x-ray technician and bacteriologist, and fifteen graduate nurses, the facility could accommodate 200 patients. The compound also housed a ballroom, cafeteria, grill, kitchen, drug store, and more—a town under one roof, as it became known. Mineral-filled swimming pools and bathhouses along with lovely grounds completed the picture.

The Phy Estate sold the facilities in 1947, and plans to convert it into a resort/retirement center began. Hot Lake Resort and Retirement Center provided nursing home care until it closed in 1974. As part of a plan to restore the property to its one-time grandeur, another owner, Stephen Munson, submitted a nomination for the resort to be listed on the National Register of Historic Places; it was so designated in 1979. The property has since been purchased with grand plans for its future.

Shirley Peters and her sister Sheila Smith researched, wrote, and published a history: *Hot Lake, The Town Under One Roof*. "Just when we think that the demise of the old Hot Lake resort is final, someone steps up to the plate to try his or her hand at reviving the past. The history of Hot Lake lives on," said Peters. "Saved from the wrecking ball, perhaps in another fifty to one hundred years the continuing saga of *Hot Lake: The Town Under One Roof* shall be written by someone else with a passion for the past."

Details: On Oregon 203 between Island City and Union, there is room to pull off the road. This is private property; you can drive into the Hot Lake RV Resort on Hot Lake Lane, where historic photos of the resort are displayed. *Hot Lake: The Town Under One Roof* can be found at the Elgin and Union museums and the Union County Chamber of Commerce.

No14 HOT LAKE SANATORIUM, HOT LAKE, OREGON

Union County

Victorian Union: After seeing the decrepit state of Hot Lake, it is nice to roll into Union, established 1862, City of Victorian Heritage, and seek out the historic homes and buildings. That's not to say they are all restored, but some gems like the Miller House, 101 E. Bryan; the Thomas Octagonal Tower House, 475 North Main; the Wright House, 429 N. Bellwood; and the beautifully restored Townley House, 782 5th, are worth the visit.

Stop by the Union County Museum on Main Street and pick up a flyer for a self-guided tour. Also on Main Street is the old Wright Opera House, now a school bus storage barn, the 1891 City Hall, Union Hotel, and the 1912 library, a gift of the Andrew Carnegie Foundation. Unfortunately, the zoning is such that the historic residential structures mingle with manufactured homes, trailers, and other newer structures.

Elgin, Where Politics and Theater Mix: When the need for a proper city hall and the condemning of the local opera house coincided, La Grande architect John Slater (who coincidentally condemned the old opera house) got the commission to design the new Colonial-

style building, built in 1912. The heart of the red brick structure was the auditorium with seating for 500 complete with a balcony, orchestra pit, box seating, hand-painted backdrops, plush draperies, a fly-loft, and a full stage for live productions and motions pictures. Flanking the front of the structure were two offices on the ground floor and a council room in the front of the second floor. The basement housed the police station and two jail cells.

The city hall is now a museum, and a wide variety of live entertainment draws crowds to the opera house. Just as the original planners envisioned it, the space is never wasted. Weddings, graduations, and a variety of events are held in the building, now listed on the National Register of Historic Places. 104 N. 8th St., (541) 437-2014 (museum), and (541) 437-3456 (opera house).

THE OREGON TRAIL, THAT 2,000-MILE stretch of rutted road and oftentimes-ruined dreams, is big business in the state. There are not one but two Oregon Trail centers in Baker City alone: The National Historic Oregon Trail Interpretive Center and the Oregon Trail Regional Museum. Other interpretive centers include The End of the Oregon Trail in Oregon City, the Columbia Gorge Discovery Center in The Dalles, and the Tanastuskujt Cultural Center on the Umatilla Indian Reservation. The Oregon Trail Advisory Council's mission is to oversee the promotion, development, and protection of the Trail. An adjunct committee, the Oregon Trail Coordinating Council, "work(s) toward interpretive development of Oregon's other national historic trails." Various nonprofit groups such as the Oregon–California Trail Association and its many volunteers are dedicated to preserving the Trail and its incredible history. The Bureau of Land Management in Oregon oversees and works with these organizations.

Ruts still remain cast in the hard barren earth for tourists to see and history buffs to preserve. Historic interpretive markers at various spots and crossings attempt to tell the story of the pioneers who traveled from the Missouri River to the Platte River, across the Continental Divide, down the Snake River to Fort Boise, then north through the Blue Mountains to northeast Oregon. Here towns like Vale have tried to put a hook on the tourism wagon train with a series of murals, and Oregon Trail monikers precede everything from cafés to T-shirt shops. There are also pageants and reenactments of the grueling trek and at least one PBS television documentary. Did I mention you can get a video game for the kiddies that

"pits players against all of the hazards a wagon-train voyage can dish out"?

The real thing began in 1841 when a small group of pioneer immigrants followed the fur traders' route; another small group did the same in 1842. But it was the massive 1843 Great Migration, a wagon train of nearly 900 people, which opened the floodgates to other groups of pioneers. Of the 300,000 who ventured west on the trail between 1840 and 1860, about 53,000 came to what is now Oregon. What they went through in the process was just plain horrendous, and it's estimated that 20,000 pioneers died in route. That doesn't include the Native Americans killed and displaced. (Contrary to folklore, most pioneers died of cholera and other diseases or by accidentally shooting each other, not at the hands of Indians.) The trail did not end in northeast Oregon. Emigrants who made it to The Dalles boated down the Columbia River or tried alternate routes such as the Barlow Road, Meek's Cutoff, and Applegate Trail. All were hazardous.

Dozens of fascinating books are in print about the Oregon Trail, but the first writings of the quest for the West, or the Manifest Destiny, were described by Capt. John Fremont, who traveled the trail in 1842 and 1843. His upbeat reports fired up easterners, who began the journey in Missouri—as they were meant to do.

So, how does one experience and learn about the Oregon Trail? First, read books, especially those with first-hand accounts. This is not to say that tourists should avoid the Oregon Trail interpretive centers, markers, and towns—quite the contrary, these can give a moving and fun experience. As part of the 150th anniversary of the famous migration, forty historic and scenic points of

interest are detailed in a self-guided tour brochure available from the Oregon Tourism Commission.

As you are driving along, look for the historic markers made of two large Port Orford cedars: these were built by the Oregon Department of Transportation in the 1940s, 1950s, and 1960s, and text is routed in panels of wood. The newer interpretive signs have color and graphics.

> **Details:** National Historic Oregon Trail Interpretive Center, Baker City, Exit 320 from Interstate 84 and follow the signs, (541) 523-1843, open daily except Thanksgiving, Christmas, and New Year's Day; Oregon Trail Regional Museum, 2480 Grove St., Baker City, (541) 523-9308, open May through October. Most towns along the trail have their own community museums, including one in Huntington.

Circle the Wagons, We're Down for the Night

Miles of the Oregon Trail follow what is now Interstate 84, and a favorite stop for the worn out, dust-encrusted pioneers was at Farewell Bend on the Idaho–Oregon border where they could water the stock and wash their clothes in a placid spot on the Snake River. Today, it is one of Oregon's lovely state parks. With a phone call, you can reserve a covered wagon for the night. Now that's the Oregon Trail of the twenty-first century!

The real wagons were 4 by 10 feet with wooden frames, linseed-treated cotton canvas covers, heavy axles, a water barrel, toolbox, and hardwood brakes. A family of four needed over a thousand pounds of food to make it through the journey, in addition to game and fish killed along the way. We stopped at a grocery store in Baker City for our supplies.

Our wagon was a re-creation of an original with a canvas canopy, wooden frame, and big stationary wheels complete with brakes. Of course, it also had two double beds and electrical outlets. Outside on the lawn was a picnic table, bundle of wood, and old-fashioned cooking pit. The foam mattresses were very comfortable, and

instead of the sound of slumbering live-stock, campers hear the slight drone of traf-fic down Interstate 84. Build a campfire, and read aloud from one of the diaries or journals, such as *Across the Plains in 1844*, by Catherine Sager Pringle.

> **Details:** Farewell Bend State Recreation Area, off Interstate 84, 25 miles northwest of Ontario; reserva-tions (541) 869-2365 or (800) 452-5687; or visit www.oregonstateparks.org. In addition to wagons, there are tepees, cabins, and campsites.

Murals of Vale

The idea of outdoor murals has turned dozens of Oregon's historic (and not his-toric) buildings into canvases for artistic interpretations of the region's significant events. Nowhere is that more evident than in Vale, where pioneers traveling northward crossed the Malheur River, then stopped and camped at the hot springs nearby. Wagon train wheel ruts can been seen up the hill at Keeney Pass, and an 1872 way station, the historic and beautifully restored Stone House (Museum), remains intact.

But it was the murals that the town was betting on to draw tourists and bolster eco-nomic development when the first mural went up in 1993. "It started because of the 150 year celebration [of the Oregon Trail]," explained Rita McGraw, director of the Heritage Reflections Mural Society. "It has made some buildings look better than they did, and exposed people to art and artists." The impact on the economy never panned out. The Society continues to commission artists to recreate gigantic interpretations of historic Trail events. Building owners have to offer the wall and prepare it for painting; the Mural Society arranges the rest.

The murals' odd contrast to 21st century life can be disconcerting. Pioneer Bank's mural includes a covered wagon that cam-ouflages the trash containers; a woman pio-neer in "The New Arrivals" looks longingly at the Dairy Queen across the street; and next to a Farmers Insurance Group sign, traders and Indians seem to be making some sort of transaction outside a tepee in the deep of winter. Even the library has a mural and inscribed above the lintel: "I must keep writing to remember who I am."—Pioneer Woman. With so many docu-mented journals of women traveling the Trail, one does wonder who she was.

> **Details:** Vale is at the junction of U.S. 20 and U.S. 26, east of Ontario.

Upper John Day River Overlook

The oversized covered wagon that looms before you on the Journey Through Time, Oregon Scenic Byway drive, makes for a good stop on U.S. 26 outside Dayville. Which brings us to drives: the Oregon Tourism Commission and Oregon Department of Transportation have available numerous maps with scenic drives. Favorites from eastern Oregon include The Wild Wild East, with spots of interest (absolutely no descrip-tions) of Grant, Harney, and Malheur coun-ties; and The Grande Tour of Union County. The Oregon Tourism Commission website is www.traveloregon.com.

Deschutes Crossing

Steelhead fishermen fill the state park campground where the Deschutes River meets the Columbia River. Standing unno-ticed is a small kiosk that gives the history of pioneers on the Oregon Trail who crossed the treacherous Deschutes at this point. The train whistle blows, trucks bar-rel down Interstate 84, motor homes fill the green lawns of the Deschutes River State Recreation Area with all of the comforts of home, and anglers await the late September steelhead run.

A rock along the highway bridge is afixed with a bronze plate:

> *To honor pioneers who with their wagons crossed The Deschutes at this place.*
> Given by Wasco Pioneers Association
> May 1937

Additional new interpretive signs installed along the river tell more of the tale. Looking down on the water, it's difficult to imagine prairie schooners being floated on barges across the river, livestock swimming, and women and children given passage in canoes navigated by Indians. After making it across the Deschutes, emigrants chose between rafting down the Columbia or opting for the Barlow Road route around Mt. Hood—neither an easy journey. Oregon Trail history continues to unfold as you travel to Hood River and then on to Cascade Locks, where the pioneers were forced to leave the river and portage their goods, long before the rapids were quieted by today's dams. Finally, river travelers who hadn't drowned or died from other accidents or disease arrived exhausted at Fort Vancouver, where they crossed the river to continue overland into the Willamette Valley.

If you missed the covered wagon campsite at Farewell Bend, there's another chance at the campground at Deschutes Crossing.

Details: From Interstate 84 take Exit 97 (Oregon 206) south to the Deschutes River State Recreation Area; www.oregonstateparks.org.

STRETCHES OF SOUTHEASTERN OREGON along the Idaho border roll out like an endless sheet of desolation. Sage-covered hills skirted by buttes and singular rock formations suddenly give way to valleys where orchards and farmland break into a patchwork of cultivated topography. Just as suddenly, it is back to the barren stretches. Then there is Succor Creek and Leslie Gulch, part of the Owyhees, a domain of ancient calderas.

Put on your pith helmets, check your water supply, and get ready for what my husband called a geologic safari. It was August, and sunflowers created a path of color along dirt-and-gravel Succor Creek Road. Cattle roamed, rabbits and lizards darted about, and we bounced. Fifteen miles into the trip, a bullet-riddled sign announced that we had reached Succor

Creek State Park. As the road dropped into the box canyon cut into lava rock, the walls looked like they had been sprayed with pastel green paint, really clay mineral deposits. The chatter of chukars broke the silence. Hundreds of the birds were in motion, making the hillside come alive.

Once in the inner gorge of the canyon, towering spires, pinnacles, mounds, and monoliths surround you. There are a few roadside pullouts at which to stop and marvel at the scene. The road climbs out of the canyon, and there is a wonderful overlook to check out just where you have ventured. Most spots like Succor Creek are accessible only by hiking trails, so this road trip truly is remarkable.

But the best is yet to come. At another remote junction, follow the 9-mile road to Leslie Gulch, named after Hiram E. Leslie, who was killed by lightning in the gulch in

Lake Owyhee State Park

The 53-mile-long Lake Owyhee was formed by the Owyhee Dam, part of the Bureau of Reclamation project to irrigate 105,000 acres in Oregon and Idaho. Though

you can access the lake by boat from the end of Leslie Gulch, you need to drive back to Oregon 201, head toward Nyssa, and turn at Owyhee Junction to enter the park. Top-notch trout fishing can be found along the river below the dam, and camping on the shores of Lake Owyhee gives visitors an opportunity for some spectacular stargazing. There are two tepees for rent at the park. Each is pitched on a deck and offers the best sites in the campground. A canoe comes with each tepee—the perfect way to see some of the geologic formations along the rim of the reservoir. The volcanic history is of the same period as Leslie Gulch: the off-white ash lay-

ers, pinkish-gray rhyolite, and deep-toned basalt have preserved plant and animal fossils. Oh, yes, there are microscopic gold particles in them thar hills.

Tepees (and campsites) are available May 1 to October 15 and can be reserved by calling (800) 452-5687; www.oregonstateparks.org.

1882. The gulch ranges from 30 to 200 feet wide and dead-ends at Owyhee Reservoir. If you closed your eyes, then opened them once you were in the gulch, you would swear you were in the canyon country of southern Utah. Baked red and terracotta colors bathe pinnacles that soar up to 2,000 feet against a background of less flashy colored cliffs. Volcanic eruptions from Mahogany Mountain to the south created layers of ash-flow tuff that were folded, flattened, then eroded beginning more than 15.5 million years ago. Gas bubbles left pock-marked tuffs, and massive rocks carried by the flow left formations like a cupped hand reaching out to hold...what?

Game trails traverse the scene. In 1965, seventeen California bighorn sheep were reintroduced into Leslie Gulch, and the herd had expanded to around 100 as of a 2002 hel-icopter survey. Mule deer and Rocky Mountain elk are also found in the area. In addition to chukars, songbirds, raptors, California quail, northern flickers, and white-throated swifts can be spotted. There are numerous reptiles including rattlesnakes. In 1983 the Bureau of Land Management designated 11,653-acre Leslie Gulch an Area of Critical Environmental Concern to protect its unique scenery, bighorn sheep habitat, and rare plant species. Yet much of the area is open to hunting.

Details: We accessed Succor Creek Rd. from the north off Oregon 201; you can also take the Succor Creek Scenic Byway off U.S. 95 north of Jordan Valley. This can be a treacherous road, and one to be avoided if it rains. Make sure your car has a high clearance, and pulling a trailer or driving an RV is not recommended.

U.S. 95 HEADING SOUTH FROM IDAHO cuts to the west around crater beds through the town of Jordan Valley toward Steens Mountain, the favored pasture of Basque sheepherders. At that axis sits a masonry and stone bit of Basque history. The open two-walled structure of native sandstone with stucco interior is a Basque fronton (handball court) that Basque sheepherders constructed in the spring of 1915. The Basques, who came to southern Oregon after the California Gold Rush, loved pelota (handball). The stone for the fronton was carted from a quarry east of Jordan Valley, hand-hewed and mortared into the 35-foot-high walls. Games were played in the afternoons and evenings, with spectators lining the right side of the court to watch competition between teams or two men.

Until the Great Depression, Basque families and their herds multiplied, and sheepherding was a major part of the Oregon

National Historic Place interpretive information. Donor pavers fill the patio with surnames like Carrica, Urquidi, Cossel, Berrojalbiz, Pascoe, Obieta, and Uria.

> **Details:** Jordan Valley is on U.S. 95, about 90 miles south of Ontario. For additional information on Basque culture, visit the Four Rivers Cultural Center and Museum in Ontario, www.4rcc.com.

economy. As sheepherding diminished, many Basques moved to towns like Jordan Valley. Although regular games haven't been played at the fronton since 1935, the Basque communities still reach deep for their roots, and festivals, interpretive sites, and food specialties keep the old traditions alive.

Part of that effort was the 1997 restoration of the 1915 fronton. The restoration—signed by Danok Etorri—has many additions from the original court, including a patio and concrete tables and chairs and

Basques

Basques in the New World: The first Basques ventured to the New World with Christopher Columbus in 1492.

Roots: In Jordan Valley, two-thirds of the population are of Basque ancestry.

Basque Country: Original Basque country is a region in northern Spain, called Vascongadas, bordered by the Pyrenees and the Bay of Biscay on the North Atlantic. Some Basques first immigrated to South America, where they raised cattle.

Why Sheepherders? Basques were not traditionally sheepherders, but when the Gold Rush did not pan out for many, they raised and herded cattle. After the California drought, the Basques saw a need for sheepherders and filled it, moving to Nevada, Idaho, and southeastern Oregon.

Basque Festivals: Bet Alai traditional dances are still performed at the Malheur County Fair and the Basque Festival at the Four Rivers Cultural Center in Ontario. The festival also features a traditional Basque dinner, traditional folk dance performance, lamb auction, and public dancing to live music.

Language: The Basques speak a language unique to the world called Euskara.

WE SET OUT TO THE MALHEUR Cemetery to find unusual tombstones from a fraternal group, the Modern Woodmen of America. We found the tombstones and the first inkling of what traveling in Oregon in the mid-1800s must have been like. Obviously, we were driving a car, not a wagon, but the miles of nothing but sage, dust, and rocks and the constant state of desolation were daunting. Of course, we had county roads to follow and dangling directional signs in our search for Malheur City (no more) and the cemetery.

There are dozens of pioneer cemeteries in the state, and each is moving, but somehow the 1870 Malheur Cemetery touched our hearts. Was the prospect of gold strong enough to settle here? And how could families survive this: the children of R. M. and M. J. Diven, each laid out with a lovely tombstone with angels and verses for four who died in succession on December 13, 21, 23, and 25, 1877.

As for the Woodmen grave markers—large tree stumps with branches and intricate tributes—they have little to do with logging or timber. In 1883, Joseph Cullen Root founded the fraternal benefit society. In 1889 there was a leadership dispute; Root left and began Woodmen of the World Life Insurance Society. At the same time, there was a third organization called Woodmen of the World Pacific Jurisdiction, now called Woodmen of the World/Assured Life Association. All of this makes the genesis of these markers a bit tricky, but according to Gail Levis, historian for Modern Woodmen of America, the Malheur markers were likely from the Pacific Jurisdiction or from Root's first fraternal Woodmen of the World, which continues today out of Omaha, Nebraska.

The original Woodmen stones were intended to follow a design sent by the home office to local stonecutters. The tree stumps, part of the fraternal organization's logo, usually stand 4–5 feet high. In the 1920s the gravestones were discontinued.

insurance companies, there are various types of Woodmen markers in Oregon, but all trace back to Joseph Cullen Root and the Sunday church sermon about pioneer woodmen that inspired him to begin the organization and call it Woodmen.

The historic markers are now fairly rare, and in some regions of the country lodge members continue to care for the grave markers and sites. The Woodmen gravesites at Malheur are of members who died in 1892, 1904, and 1906. The motto of the fraternal group: "No Woodmen shall rest in an unmarked grave," no matter how desolate the area. With the various offshoots of the fraternal organization and

Details: Exit U.S. 26 at Ironside (if coming from the west) or Brogan (if coming from the east), and follow signs to Malheur Reservoir (Willow Creek Rd.) to Huntington Junction (a fork in the road), then to Mormon Basin. You will also pass what is left of a stone shelter originally built into the side of the hill. The cemetery is on the top of a hill, easily seen because it is the only greenery for miles.

THE KAM WAH CHUNG & CO. MUSEUM stands as a time capsule. Not the metal tube–type stuffed with memorabilia to be opened on a designated day in the future, this small museum is a cultural treasure,

and the best small museum that I've seen in Oregon. And it wasn't planned as such. The museum is a step back to time spanning between 1887 and 1948, when the doors were locked on the Chinese general store and herbalist's office. Also locked behind those doors was the social touchstone to the Chinese miners who flooded to the region beginning in the late 1800s. With one large Buddhist shrine, a kitchen god shrine, and a smaller shrine, it served as a make-do temple. Each day the main shrine's Three Precious Things—wine,

fruit, and incense—were replaced, and worshippers turned to Ing Hay for spiritual guidance. Dry goods business and medicine along with hiring, translating, cooking, gambling, prohibition era bootlegging, and opium (legal until 1909) were practiced here, and remnants of each collected since the establishment opened in 1887 stand where they were left.

The building was originally constructed in 1866/67 as a trading post on The Dalles Military Road. In 1887, Ing Hay and Lung On bought the building, where they lived and worked until they left in 1948 and 1940, respectively. "Doc" Hay and Lung On emigrated from China, but they had been established in Walla Walla, Washington, prior to moving to John Day. These two gentlemen created the hub of the Chinese community in John Day while becoming entrepreneurs, civic leaders, and in Doc Hay's case a trusted and respected herbalist and doctor. Lung On was the polished and poised businessman who could translate for members of the Chinese community, and his friend of fifty-three years, Ing Hay, was the perfect business partner.

Lung On died suddenly in 1940, and Doc Hay died in 1952. The Kam Wah Chung & Co. Building was deeded to the City of John Day with the provision that it be made into a museum, as instructed by Ing Hay. For over a decade it sat with both men's personal belongings, herbal medicines, antiques, books, shrines, and calendars preserved in the old stone building. In 1967, while the city was surveying the land around the store for a city park, the city fathers found that they owned the Kam Wah Chung building and its contents. With the help of the National Trust for Historic Preservation, the Oregon State Parks Bureau, and the Oregon Historical Society along with students and faculty from the University of Oregon and Lewis and Clark College and the efforts of local volunteers, the building was restored, cleaned, and inventoried, and then everything was replaced as it had been in 1940.

Oregon Parks and Recreation Department owns the museum building, which is managed by the City of John Day. The building is listed on the National Register of Historic Places.

Details: The museum is in John Day City Park on Canton St. and is clearly marked on U.S. 26. Call (541) 575-0028 for hours.

WE TOOK THE MITCHELL BUSINESS EXIT off U.S. 26 and pulled into town. A Labor Day festival was wrapping up, and since the chairs were still out and the sound system in place, church services were being held in the city park instead of inside the stuffy sanctuary. We ate breakfast at the Little Pine Café, a no-nonsense spot where breakfast is served all day and a rifle to be auctioned by the Lions Club hung over the cash register. Catrina Welty took our order and, with the hash and eggs, also gave us a little information about who owned the bear, Henry, who lives in a cage in the middle of town.

Mitchell is one of those historic ranching towns (established in 1863) that can only surprise visitors. And Henry and Hugh were the surprises of the day. Hugh Reed owns the gas station in the center of town (he used to own the café, too). Behind the pumps is a large zoolike enclosure. I looked through the fence at the habitat of huge boulders, a pond, log den, and straw and wondered where was the bear? It seemed that within minutes, instead of wondering, I was feeding cookies to a 450-pound, 4-year-old bear as he lounged on the rock next to his master, Hugh...and me. By the way, Hugh is a bear of a man himself.

Hugh sort of inherited Henry when he was a year old after the Boys Club that bought him (and had him neutered and declawed) didn't want him anymore. According to Hugh, you had to pay to get a zoo to take the animal, and anyway, Hugh was getting attached to the American black bear. "He's my buddy now," said Hugh, as he gave the bear a, well, bear hug. Buckets of apples, carrots, and dog food are Henry's daily staples. He's "only a teenager," said Hugh, and the expectation is that Henry will top 700 pounds. Hugh does all of the

feeding (my cookie feeding was an exception to the rule), hoping that Henry will only take food that Hugh has touched. Someone tried to poison Henry once, so Hugh takes all the precautions he can to

protect the bear. The cookie treat finished, Henry did a few lazy well-intentioned tricks, then sauntered back into his den to sleep. Hugh got back to pumping gas for the camouflaged hunters (it was the opening of bow season), and we walked down Main Street.

Though Mitchell's Main Street is only a few blocks long, there are other spots worth mentioning. First, the Visitor Center, the kind of place folks who have been hunting or camping would welcome: there is a shower ($2), restrooms (free), and coin-operated washer and dryer. You can help yourself to

tourism brochures, too. The Oregon Hotel, a nice looking spot to hang your hat; the Wheeler County Trading Co., the local general store; the old Mitchell State Bank, where the name and year, 1918, are found in the slab in front of the entry; and the park are all pleasant. If you're lucky, Elizabeth Carroll will come out of her house and chat with you about Mitchell's history.

There's a lovely cemetery outside of town with pioneer plots that attest to the town's history. More recently, Mitchell, built in a narrow spot in Bridge Creek Canyon, has been the victim of a series of devastating flashfloods.

> **Details:** Mitchell is about halfway between Prineville and John Day on U.S. 26 in Wheeler County.

THE RED BRICK WHEELER COUNTY Courthouse in the cattle and timber town of Fossil opened in 1901 after some jostling over what town would house the county seat. Fossil won out, and architect Charles Burggaf was commissioned to design the building with its turret and observation

Oregon where the business of its original intent is conducted. The courthouse stands as a lovely and substantial reminder of the region's past.

So, what about the teapots across the lane? For 20 years, Doug and Bettie Elder's home and yard have been the haven for

The yard is bordered by 108 teapots, and Doug suspects there are about 170 displayed on their property. And if there's one thing that says volumes about Fossil, it might be that the Elders have never had one teapot stolen.

tower; it was constructed for just over $9,000. Fossil's name was coined when the first postmaster discovered fossil remains on his property—not surprising since the marvelous John Day Fossil Beds layer many square miles of Wheeler County.

Today, Fossil has about 400 residents and the courthouse is one of only two in

teapots from around the world. "It started with three or four teapots," explained Doug Elder as he surveyed the eclectic landscaping. "My wife started it and people started buying them and leaving them on the porch or sending them here. We got one addressed to The Teapot Lady, Teapot Lane, Fossil, Oregon. It got here."

Location: Fossil is at the junction of Oregon 218 and Oregon 19; Wheeler County Courthouse, 701 Adams St.; Teapot House, 310 Adams St.

THERE ARE HUNDREDS OF GOLF courses in Oregon, and high-end golf resorts and communities continue to gobble up the arid countryside east of the Cascades. In what looks like one proud step for land use, the six-hole Kinzua Hills Golf Club ranks as the shortest course in the state. Each hole has three sets of tees (with horseshoe tee markers), so you can play eighteen holes by play-

visit was full of coolers and cold cuts. A group of golfers from John Day had loaded their electric carts on flatbed trucks and made a day outing to Kinzua. At $5 for six holes, $10 for twelve, and $15 for eighteen holes, it's a popular spot for thrifty golfers. Family memberships run $150. A campground with motor homes and RVs becomes a permanent "village" during the summer.

Details: Finding Kinzua Hills Golf Club can be more challenging than the course. From Fossil, go south on Main St. to the Oregon 19 intersection and follow signs to Spray–John Day. Turn left at the Kinzua–Lone Rock junction at a metal piece of "art": a flying motorcycle rider careening off his bike. Continue 3 miles, turn left after the Thirty Mile Creek crossing, and follow the Kinzua Golf Club signs. We entered from the other side and took one of our great unplanned side trips, finally dumping out at Oregon 207 where we made our way to Heppner.

ing the course three times. Kinzua is also one of the most remote courses in the state.

Off a dirt road in the Umatilla National Forest, near the appropriately named Lost Valley, you just have to ask yourself what is a golf course doing out here? The 1930 era course was the brainchild of the owner and employees of Kinzua Pine Mills Co. The company town and mill are gone, but the golf course—after a stint as a baseball field— remains. The logging past can still be seen off the second fairway, where cattails fill what was once the millpond. This is open-range cattle country, so it's not uncommon to share the links with four-legged duffers. The clubhouse is a basic affair with a front porch and picnic area, which during my

The course marshal, manager, greenskeeper, and self-proclaimed "flunky," Pat Bunyard, tends Kinzua Hills. There are 120 family memberships out of the county, and the course gets "lots of open play" on a first-come, first-served basis. Golfers pay by the honor system, signing up and dropping their fees in a box nailed to the clubhouse. "It's a tough little course," says Bunyard. Not as tough as caring for it. In August 2003, the course lost its right to privately owned reservoir water, and Bunyard was hauling water for the greens and tee boxes. The temperature was hovering at 90 degrees; Bunyard was shaking his head as folks were teeing off at every box in golflike bliss.

What Happened to Kinzua?

I was actually looking for the company town of Kinzua when we found the golf course. Golf, yes; town, no. Kinzua may be on the map, but that's it.

Life was flush in this company town, according to a 1968 Crow's Forest Products newsletter: "Located in Oregon's remote east-central country, Kinzua is just about as far away from anywhere as you can get without falling clear off the map. But this little island on the Oregon high plateau has just about everything many little towns have and a heck of a lot more than most." One of the state's "company towns," Kinzua was established in 1928, a year after Kinzua Pine Mills Co. opened its ponderosa pine mill. The community included 125 homes, a church, recreation hall (which served as a skating rink, theater, union meeting hall, and dance hall) with café, tavern, barber shop, library, post office, company general store, and school. A common-carrier railroad hauled supplies and passengers to Condon. Early on, Kinzua printed its own money for use in the company stores, café, and, of course, tavern. The mill employed 330 workers, and at one time Kinzua was the biggest town in Wheeler County.

Kinzua moved its mill operation to Heppner in 1953, and the town and mill were sold to new owners. The railroad's last run was in 1976, and the mill and logging operations continued there until 1978. Kinzua was then dismantled and carted away.

Southern Oregon

Upper Klamath Lake

Crater Lake may be Oregon's only national park, but the public land of the southern portion of the state is ripe with other spectacular, oftentimes overlooked, scenic treasures. For birders this is paradise, with flyways creating heavenly interstates full of the rare and the regular of the bird world. Road warriors usually cross the state on Highway 97 or Interstate 5, but one-of-kind experiences await those who follow Oregon's Outback Scenic Byway, turn onto one of a dozen small dirt roads, or stop at the tiny towns that dot the region.

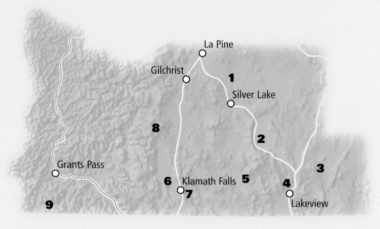

1 Big Hole, Hole in the Ground, Fort Rock
2 Summer Lake
3 Abert Rim
4 Old Perpetual
5 Balloon Bomb Site, Bly Ranger Station
6 Upper Klamath Lake
7 Klamath Brigade Bucket
8 Crater Lake National Park
9 Oregon Caves National Monument

THE ROMANCE OF THE AUSTRALIAN Outback may have inspired the Oregon Tourism Commission to use the name for the sweeping terrain of south-central Oregon. Roads roll over miles of trance-inducing landscape where the light transforms alkali lakebeds into mirages. The rhythm of traveling through the Outback is soulful in its solitude, and every dozen miles or so there is something that makes you squint and look more closely. This isolated rural country is mainly in Lake County. Naturally, with a name like that one would think Minnesota. Not even close.

The actual Outback Scenic Byway begins in La Pine at the junction of U.S. 97 and Oregon 31 and follows the latter until it merges with U.S. 395 at Valley Falls, then on south to Lakeview and the California border.

Just the names give you an idea of what was going on here during early Pleistocene times: Big Hole (not to be confused with Hole in the Ground), Crack in the Ground, Fort Rock, Table Rock, Abert Ridge...the list goes on. And there are more than geologic wonders out here: the ranchers, birders, environmentalists, even hunters combine their interests and efforts in creating real intrigue in Oregon's Outback.

Big Hole

Yep, that's a big hole. The quarter-mile-wide, 300-foot-deep hole was created by a huge maar (below ground level) volcanic explosion. This hole is filled with trees.

> **Details:** South off Oregon 31, 20 miles from La Pine.

Hole in the Ground

This is the empty variety of Big Hole: no trees. Actually, the nearly circular maar volcano was within a lake that filled what is now called the Fort Rock Basin. Geologists say the crater was formed in a few days or weeks by a series of explosions. The same sort of explosion outside the lake basin resulted in a cinder cone like those familiar landmarks around Bend—Pilot Butte and Lava Butte.

> **Details:** A 2–3-mile drive on a dirt road northwest off Oregon 31 on a clearly marked Forest Service road.

Fort Rock and Crack in the Ground

Again, there is nothing subtle in the names. A magnificent maar volcanic and tuff ring with wave-cut cliffs rises as a rust-colored "fort" on the sage-covered desert. What Ayers Rock is to Australia's Outback, Fort Rock is to Oregon's Outback. I prefer to admire the volcanic sculpting of Fort Rock from afar, but on my first visit we decided to climb around the caves in the horseshoe-shaped fort (eroded by Fort Rock Lake), where signs of early man were discovered in 1938 with the unearthing of 9,000-year-old woven sandals thought to be the oldest shoes on record. The discovery was made by archaeologist Luther S. Cressman and a team of University of Oregon students. In the 1960s, Cressman and U of O graduate student Stephen Bedwell made four additional archeological finds that dated human habitation of Oregon's Great Basin from 11,000 to 13,000 years ago.

Fort Rock Cave is a National Historic Landmark; the man who made it famous, Luther Cressman, died in 1994 at the age of 96.

A 12 mile drive northeast of Fort Rock gets you to Crack in the Ground. Unlike the average crack in the ground, this one—2 miles long and averaging 70 feet deep—has never been filled in by dirt or other debris. You can hike the length of it, but be prepared for ice and temperatures 20 degrees less than on the surface.

> **Details:** Follow signs off Oregon 31 east onto the Christmas Valley Byway. The Fort Rock State Park Monument is not at Fort Rock but a mile or so away.

Silver Lake

You can find out anything about a small town at the post office or, if you're lucky, the library. In Silver Lake these two facilities share the same parking lot, so it's one-stop information. Silver Lake (the lake) is no more. But the small general store, gas station, post office (established in 1874/75), library, Fremont Forest Service ranger station, empty stone school house, and cemetery are enough to warrant a stop. That's because what happened in Silver Lake in 1894 put it on the map.

By 1894, fifteen blocks of the town had been platted, where a blacksmith shop, feed barn, a couple of general merchandise stores, saloon, and homes were built. On Christmas Eve, most everyone from town and the surrounding ranches gathered in Clayton Hall for holiday festivities. The 150 or so people got settled, and, as the program wrapped up, a man in the audience knocked a hanging lamp that burst into flames. Mayhem ensued, and firsthand accounts before the coroner's jury described a horrendous scene of children being trampled, families being burned, and people being dragged through two small windows from the frame structure only to stand out-side and watch their neighbors burn. Forty people died that night and three more afterward. No family was left untouched.

None of the remains could be identified, so the ashes were gathered and buried in caskets in a common grave. In 1898, a large stone monument was brought from Eugene to the Silver Lake Cemetery. The huge marker, with the forty-three names, stands today.

> **Details:** Silver Lake is on Oregon 31, about 18 miles south of the Fort Rock turnoff. The cemetery can be seen from the highway just outside of town heading toward Summer Lake.

Summer Lake

The great surprise at Summer Lake was not so much that the 60-square-mile lake seemed nearly empty when we were there in September, but that there is such joy in watching birds—275 species of birds: white pelicans, herons, ibis, swans, ducks (39,000 on the day we were there), even owls. When the snow geese migration comes in late February and March and again in late fall, there can be 100,000 birds filling the sky and marsh. This is a birder's paradise, where two-legged oglers can experience an unparalleled look at the winged friends that share this planet.

The Summer Lake Wildlife Area, under the jurisdiction of the Oregon Department of Fish and Wildlife, is a 18,700-acre marsh and uplands area with an 8.3-mile tour route that you can drive or hike. Millions of waterfowl and shorebirds use it as a rest spot or place to mate. Early spring is the premiere time to view migrating flocks of waterfowl; early March through April ducks and shorebirds, especially swans and snow geese, can be viewed; April and May are good times to see songbirds and resident or migrant waterfowl. The sunrises are spectacular, and the sunsets make a less showy exit behind Winter Ridge. The names Summer Lake and Winter Ridge came thanks to Capt. John C. Fremont, who in 1843 looked down at the lake from the ridge and, due to the contrast, came up with the names.

degree water of Old Perpetual was directed through a casing. The geyser used to erupt about twice a minute; today, Old Perpetual spouts every four to five minutes. If you're thinking Old Faithful in Yellowstone, you'll be disappointed.

Incidentally, Oregon is volcanic, so there's quite a bit still going on down under. That includes dozens of hot springs, and many are open to the public. Some you wouldn't pay me to get into, but others are quite nice and have been developed into resorts. If you're looking for hot springs on the internet, it's best to get on a site with photographs. Most of the hot springs are in southern and eastern Oregon, and there is another batch in the Cascades.

Early October through late January is hunting season, and the silence is broken not by the honks of the goose horn section and staccato of chirping songbirds but by the sound of gunfire. The tour route is closed during hunting season.

There are a couple of places to hang your binoculars while at Summer Lake: the funky and fun Lodge at Summer Lake directly across from the Wildlife Area entrance, or Summer Lake Inn, where the birders sip wine outside their board-and-batten cottages. Campsites are also available along the Wildlife Area Tour Route.

> **Details:** Summer Lake Wildlife Area is on Oregon 31, about 70 miles from La Pine if you come from the north or 7 miles from Paisley to its south.

Abert Rim

U.S. 395 and Oregon 31 merge at Valley Falls south of Summer Lake; thrust along the byway is the largest exposed geologic fault scrap in North America. For 30 miles along U.S. 395 as you head north toward

Burns, Abert Rim rises 2,500 feet above Lake Abert to its west, while the eastern slope falls into Warner Valley. Captain Fremont visited the lake and rim in 1843 and wrote of it in his diaries. The lake and rim were named for Col. F. F. Abert, Chief of the Topographical Bureau, the man Fremont reported to on this expedition.

Old Perpetual Geyser

Lake County is full of hot springs, but most keep close to the ground. Just outside Lakeview is Oregon's only regularly spouting geyser, which began spewing in 1923 near Hunter's Hot Springs.

In the 1920s sanatoriums around hot springs were the vogue. Dr. H. A. Kelly and his associates, including financier H. A. Hunter, decided that the hot springs just north of Lakeview would be a good spot to test the waters of therapeutic treatment while incorporating a destination resort meant to lure wealthy tourists to this remote timber and cattle town. Part of the project involved drilling that garnered three geysers. Of the three, only one continued. The 180

> **Details:** Old Perpetual is just off U.S. 395 north of Lakeview at Hunter's Hot Springs Resort.

ALONG A STRETCH OF U.S. 97, ABOUT 50 miles south of Bend and a mile north of Crescent, appears a village coated in dark chocolate brown. On one side of the highway, a broad lawn blankets the landscape with houses arranged in a camplike setting along the Little Deschutes River. Farther north stands a small shopping mall and theater. Tucked into the pines above the shopping mall (the first of its kind in the state) are

town business instead of Gilchrist Timber Company, and retirees and second home-owners live side-by-side with mill workers. Each of the changes says something about present-day Gilchrist. Change has become Gilchrist's middle name.

The dam, sawmill, powerhouse, and log pond along with rail lines were running or under construction when Portland town planner and architect Hollis Johnston gave

harvesting, downing individual trees rather than clear-cutting swathes of forest. The timber was then processed at their own mill.

As for the company town, Mr. Johnston had a pristine slate to work with and approached the job with the site's integrity in mind. His goal was to create a town "approaching the ideal of the best town planning thought as nearly as possible." The town would include homes on varying

the original company houses and cottages. The shopping mall, theater, and riverside buildings still feature the traditional brown paint job and Scandinavian rosemal detailing that gave the town the nickname Brown Town. The homes above the mall sport new pastel vinyl siding and metal roofs; the old church (originally the company commissary) is now Ernst Brothers LLC and a real estate office. A homeowners' association manages

his recommendation for the company town to Frank W. Gilchrist. Gilchrist came from a line of savvy shipping and lumber business-men who over the years had acquired forests in central Oregon. In 1937 the Gilchrist-Fordney Company left its Mississippi operation and moved here to the 100,000-acre forests full of old-growth ponderosa pines, forming Gilchrist Timber Company. The company's logging philosophy was selective

sized lots tucked into the forest on the hill-side on the east side of the highway. Since the location was so remote, Johnston included stores, restaurants, and social centers like a bowling alley and movie theater. Everything was worked into the existing forest, and everything was painted brown. The company owned and rented the homes to workers, whose responsibility it was to pay for the water and electricity.

After 50 years, the 500 residents still resided in the 135 houses owned and maintained by the company. Then Gilchrist went up for sale—lock, stock, mill, and movie theater.

In 1991, Crown Pacific Partners bought the Gilchrist mill and property; they weren't interested in the town, so Ernst Brothers LLC purchased the town from Crown Pacific and made plans to sell it.

Since the town of Gilchrist was on one lot, the property was platted, the homes refurbished and put on the market. The first home was sold in December 1996, according to Gil Ernst, grandson of Frank W. Gilchrist. But it is the early days that those who remain in Gilchrist like to think about: "Folks used to just pull off the road [Highway 97], put out a blanket and have a picnic on the lawn," explained Kathryn

Poncil, as she stood in front of her Gilchrist-brown cottage along the Little Deschutes. This parklike setting, designed by Johnston to be a travel trailer park, is where the Gilchrists and their extended family built their homes, homes for those hired to help them, dorms for the "single men," chicken coop, and various buildings. And this is where Mrs. Poncil and her husband, Ernest, have lived and worked for 44 years. "A friend talked us into coming here and we haven't gotten away."

The compound is still home to Mary Gilchrist Ernst, her son Gil Ernst, and his family. Gil Ernst grew up in Gilchrist. "It was great. I never thought about having kids anywhere else. I went away for awhile, then was fortunate enough to come back."

Gilchrist has the distinction of being Oregon's last company town.

Crescent

When Gilchrist was constructed, Crescent was a tiny burg with a few cabins and a school just a mile south. Today there are a couple of not-to-be-missed spots. If you have an aversion to dead animals on walls, don't stop at the Mohawk Restaurant and Lounge. But if you consider taxidermy an art form or just want to get a close look at a set of fawns taken from their deceased mommies (while they were still in the womb), do stop. Many of these animals would be found in natural history museums, since they are

endangered. There is also the obligatory two-headed calf. Even with the "Please Do Not Feed the Animals" sign over the fireplace, it's an unusual place to feed yourself while taking in a little local history. Most of these animals were found as "road kill" or given to the owners, who took care of mounting them. The collection was complete in the 1960s.

Two doors away is Ken's Sporting Goods, topped by what Ken called the Biggest Bear in the West. That would be the 15-foot carved wood bear with a 6-foot fish. Ken Jordan bought the bear in 1994 when he expanded his business. Ken is deceased, but he left quite a legacy.

CRATER LAKE IS THE CALLING CARD OF the state's most famous volcanic eruption. That volcanic story is the crux of Oregon's only national park. The eruption that formed the lake 7,700 years ago was epic, and the blast blew ash and pumice over what would become eight states and three Canadian provinces. Eventually, the whole structure of the mountain failed, cracks began to form in a ring around the edge of the mountain, and the peak collapsed, leaving a huge basin. Over time, snow and rain filled the caldera, creating Crater Lake.

There are many versions of the legends of the Mt. Mazama eruption, but Klamath Indian people's story tells of two chiefs, "Llao of the Below World" and "Skell of the Above World," who became pitted in a battle that resulted in the destruction of Llao's home, Mt. Mazama. That massive destruction created Crater Lake.

The caldera spans more than 6 miles at its widest point, and sonar surveys have calculated its maximum depth at 1,958 feet.

The intense blue color of the lake is attributed to its clarity and depth. There are no inlets; rain and snow fill the caldera while evaporation and seepage keep it in balance.

From the time John Wesley Hillman called it the bluest lake he had ever seen, people have been taken aback by the color. That blue is created as the pure water absorbs the reds, yellows, and greens of sunlight, leaving behind the blue that so permanently impresses everyone who sees it. But the lake is not an endless azure waterscape. Soon after the collapse, minor eruptions created formations like Wizard Island.

By mid-July, when the snow has finally been cleared, a 33-mile road that first opened in 1940 offers a route around the rim. Rim Drive's two-hour trip holds dozens of pullouts with magnificent views of the lake. One side road off Rim Drive on the east side of the lake takes visitors to the Pinnacles Overlook, where interpretative stations explain how thousands of years of erosion created this bizarre stand of hollow pumice spires.

For those who enjoy hiking, 140 miles of trails open up a world of wildflowers, forests of hemlock and red fir, grassy meadows, springs, canyons, and mountaintop vistas. More than fifty types of mammals make their home at the park, including snowshoe hares, mule deer, Roosevelt elk, bobcats, and a few dozen black bears. The northern spotted owl and American bald eagles are among the species in the park listed as "threatened" under the Endangered Species Act.

The park's historic architecture is a chapter in its cultural story. Crater Lake Lodge is located at Rim Village on the south side of the caldera, and 3 miles south of that is park headquarters with the historic administrative offices, ranger station, visitor center, and staff housing; a historic rehabilitation project is under way.

Although the Crater Lake Lodge is closed from mid-October to the end of May, the park is open year-round, and cross-country skiers and snowshoers—undaunted by over 500 inches of snow that falls each winter—revel in the beauty. Still, it is the lake in the summer that is the park's main draw.

Today, 500,000 visitors come each year, step to the edge of the rim, and take in the wonder of it all.

Details: Oregon 138 off U.S. 97 to the Park's north entrance; Oregon 62 to the south entrance and Park headquarters. The north entrance is typically closed from mid-October to mid-June. Crater Lake Lodge and Mazama Village Motor Inn, (541) 830-8700 for reservation information.

UPPER KLAMATH LAKE WASHES ACROSS the landscape like ice-blue paint poured over miles of wetlands, created when the earth's crust dropped along fault lines. Saddle Mountain lifts to the east of the lake, and the summit of Mt. McLoughlin looms on the west. There are days when Oregon's largest body of fresh water seems at peace. Then there are other days when the lake visually lifts itself into the sky. One minute thousands of waterfowl cover the glassy surface, and then a mass of birds take their cue and, in a moment it seems, are gone in a rush of flapping wings that leaves you stunned.

The 22-mile-long lake may cover a huge landmass, but its mean depth is only 8 feet. The lake is part of the 15,000-acre Upper Klamath Basin National Wildlife Refuge, which in turn is part of the massive 190,000-acre Klamath Basin National Wildlife

Refuges complex that encompasses protected lands in both southern Oregon and northern California. Within that area, Upper Klamath Lake, Lower Klamath Lake, Tule Lake, the Klamath River, forests, marshes, and farmland along with the forces of humans and nature attempt to coexist.

The Upper Klamath Refuge, which includes Upper Klamath Lake and adjoining Agency Lake, was established in 1928. California's Lower Klamath Refuge has the distinction of being this nation's first waterfowl refuge, established by President Theodore Roosevelt in 1908.

The Klamath Basin is the stopover for millions migrating birds of the Pacific Flyway between Alaska and Mexico, including, from December to February, the largest collection of bald eagles in the lower forty-eight states. More than 260 bird species

have been seen in the Klamath Basin, and three of the West's remaining breeding colonies of white pelicans are located at Upper and Lower Klamath and Clear Lake refuges. Two endangered fish species, the Lost River and shortnose suckers, are found in the Upper and Lower Klamath Lakes.

The Basin is also home to 220,000 acres of farmland authorized by Congress beginning in 1905 as part of the Bureau of Reclamation's Klamath Project: a network of diversion canals, dams, and levees drained and rerouted the lakes and wetlands water to be used to irrigate crops. A low dam was built on the Link River in 1917, and Upper Klamath waters were regulated from that dam. Farms expanded after World War I and II, when returning GIs were offered "homesteads" on the arid land, and the construction of the Klamath Project

was completed in 1957. The high desert became farmland, and 80 percent of the wetlands surrounding Upper Klamath Lake were altered. The stage was set for conflict.

The Endangered Species Act was passed in 1973 and the Lost River and shortnose suckers listed in 1988; the Klamath tribes

were working to protect Upper Klamath Lake and coho salmon; lobbying by noted conservation groups and farmers and dozens of scientific and government agencies became intense. These all combined to bring the water of the Upper Klamath to more than one table. By 1992 the U.S. Fish and Wildlife Service had set a minimum water level in Upper Klamath Lake. That was followed by two droughts. Things came to a head in April 2001, when the Bureau of Reclamation shut off the irrigation water to a portion of the Klamath Project's farms, along with Basin's wildlife refuges.

By May 2001, farmers had organized well-publicized events including a "Bucket Brigade" (see p. 82) in Klamath Falls, where 13,000 people protested the shut-off. Various farm and ranch organizations in Oregon and

California, including the Klamath Water Users Association, were formed.

By the end of 2003, the Bureau of Reclamation was continuing work under the National Environmental Policy Act on an environmental impact statement for the Klamath Project and seeking input on creating a "water bank"; the U.S. Department of Fish and Wildlife, Klamath Basin Ecosystem Restoration Office, implemented 271 projects; private and public sector partnerships purchased tens of thousands of acres of marsh and wetlands to conserve or restore...and the list goes on.

The waterfowl continue their flight, gracing Upper Klamath Lake with their presence and beauty. And people continue to live, work, conserve, and repair what has been done.

Details: U.S. 97 and Oregon 140 take motorists along each edge of Upper Klamath Lake and intersect at Klamath Falls. Highway 140 is part of the Volcanic Legacy Byway.

In and Around the Lake

Significant Species: The American bald eagle, American white pelican, red-necked and eared grebes, osprey, Canada goose, pintail, mallard, gadwall, canvasback, black tern, great blue heron, great egret, and snow egret are all found in the Upper and Lower Klamath Refuge, as are the endangered Lost River sucker and shortnose sucker. In addition to birds and fish, beavers, muskrats, and river otters inhabit the marshes and rivers.

Canoe Trail: This trail is easy on the legs but hard on the arms. The 9.5-mile waterway trail weaves through the Upper Klamath Marsh and is the best way to appreciate the wildlife. Enter the trail off Oregon 140 on the west side of the lake. Canoes can access the trail from either Rocky Point or Malone Spring boat launches. For information on canoe rentals at Rocky Point Resort, call (541) 356-2287.

Blue-green Algae Farming: Since the 1980s, the harvesting of *Aphanizomenon flos-aquae*, a species of blue-green algae, has been a small but controversial business, with annual harvests of 2–5 million wet pounds. The algae are thought to have nutritional benefits as a supplement but also adverse effects on the lake.

Rocky Road: No matter the season, the 10-mile stretch of U.S. 97 along Upper Klamath Lake is a heart-racing drive. The Refuge offers some of the best birdwatching in the Pacific Northwest, but you need to keep your eyes on the road. Drivers can't ignore the mile-long 10-foot-high chain-link fence holding back the cliff along the highway. According to the Oregon Department of Transportation, about fifteen accidents a year are attributed to rock versus vehicle. Then there's the railway track tucked between the highway and the marsh with its own alarm system—fencelike strings of wires that don't stop the errant boulders but do signal oncoming trains of trouble on the track. Of course, the two-lane road has to be winding just to add to the excitement.

IF A 15-FOOT-HIGH SILVER BUCKET plopped in front the Government Center on Main Street in Klamath Falls seems odd, you weren't around in the spring of 2001 when the federal government cut off irrigation water to 200,000 acres of farmland in the Klamath Basin. On May 7, 2001, a month after the water stopped, 13,000 farmers from around the West met in Klamath Falls and lifted fifty buckets of water (symbolizing a bucket per state) from the Link River in town to the dry canal that once irrigated crops. Event organizers said bucket brigades had been a symbol of shoulder-to-shoulder resolve in communities of the American West for decades.

Klamath County Commissioner John Elliott explained that the display of the bucket in front of the Government Center was "accepted not just as a symbol of farmers, but we feel it symbolizes water in the West. Our point of allowing it here is to remind everyone of the need for balance."

The moniker Bucket Brigade became The Klamath Bucket Brigade, Inc., for the purpose of sponsoring the Klamath Relief Convoys to "spread the message of the plight of the Klamath Basin farmers and ranchers"; the Klamath Relief Fund was in turn set up to disburse funds collected from the convoys.

Details: The Klamath Brigade Bucket is at 305 Main St., Klamath Falls, off U.S. 97. The Klamath Falls bucket is not alone; there is a "traveling" bucket that goes with speakers to various agricultural shows and functions.

KLAMATH BUCKET BRIGADE

ELKO TO KLAMATH
NV UT ID OR

DURING WORLD WAR II, OREGONIANS had reason to worry about their safety. Bunkers, blimps, and barricades dotted the Pacific Coast, but it was more than 200 miles from the coast in the Fremont National Forest where the only deaths on the American continent resulted from an enemy attack during the war.

Six picnickers were killed on May 5, 1945, when curiosity got the best of them. After a month of government secrecy on the subject, a minister at the picnic where the tragedy happened was allowed to tell the story to the press. He relayed the tale of a massive grayish balloon, 33 feet in diameter, found near the picnic site. The balloon, with ball bombs suspended beneath, had landed in the forest; the bombs failed to explode. The purpose of the bomb balloons, deployed by the Japanese Navy, was to start forest fires. A group on a church picnic was exploring the odd balloon when it blew up.

A large stone marker surrounded by a chain-link fence commemorates the tragedy. The names of those lost are chiseled into the stone: the eldest person was Elise Mitchell, age 26; the youngest was 11 years old. The spot is now called the Mitchell Recreation Area.

Details: Take Oregon 140 a mile east of Bly and turn left on Campbell Rd. (difficult to read since the sign is riddled with bullet holes); then take a right on Natl FS 34 and go about 9 miles. After stopping at the Mitchell memorial, continue on this paved road for a beautiful route to Paisley.

Bly Ranger Station Compound

The U.S. Forest Service Station in Bly on Oregon 140 between Klamath Falls and Lakeview is good place to stop on your way to the Mitchell memorial. The Bly Ranger Station compound is one of the best extant examples of Civilian Conservation Corps Forest Service construction in the state. The compound, on the National

Register of Historic Places, exemplifies the rustic architecture favored by both the National Park Service and the Forest Service. The Ranger Station Office, built in 1937 for $1,700, is open to the public. (Check out the scrapbook on the Mitchell bomb tragedy at the front desk.) Six additional stone buildings and stone fencing complete this architectural oasis.

Guard Residence: Built in 1942 at a cost of $1,600; has served as a residence for Forest Service personnel.

Ranger's Residence: Built in 1937 at a cost of $2,400. Today this residence is lived in by Bly District personnel.

Gas and Oil House: Once a gas and oil house, always a gas and oil house. Built in 1939 at a cost of $300.

AFTER TRAVELING UP 20 MILES OF perhaps the windiest road in southern Oregon to Oregon Caves National Monument, you're probably looking for the cave. But what's this? Buildings covered in bark? Yes, that's Port Orford cedar bark dressing one of the state's true architectural

treasures: the Chateau at Oregon Caves, a National Historic Landmark, and the smaller Chateau, part of a Swiss-inspired village. The most bark-covered structure you've probably seen before is maybe a birdhouse.

The story of this tiny monument began in 1874, when Elijah Davidson discovered a magnificent cave deep in the Siskiyou Mountains of southern Oregon. Groups of locals began crawling into the bowels of the cave with candles and torches, uncoiling ropes behind them so they could find their way out. The smell of money soon prompted small outfitters and miners to take out mineral claims around the cave and put

together expeditions to explore them. Trails were cut, a cabin constructed, and development pondered.

In 1906, the Siskiyou National Forest was established, and the land around the caves was withdrawn from mineral entry the following year, saving the caves from the ravages of mining. On July 12, 1909, the 480-acre site was set aside as one of the country's first national monuments. The proclamation read: "Any use of the land which interferes with its preservation or protection as a National Monument is hereby forbidden."

In 1909, *Sunset* magazine ran an article by Joaquin Miller about Oregon's "Marble Halls," further oiling the wheels of tourism. A road opened to the caves in 1922, and the U.S. Forest Service drafted plans for cottages as well as electrical lighting and steel ladders in the cave.

Back in Grants Pass, a group of businessmen formed the Oregon Caves Company

and began planning an exquisite colony of buildings. They hired noted Oregon landscape architect Alfred Peck to put their ideas into a plan. It was Peck's vision to create this alpine village and cover the buildings in shaggy bark. Not only was the idea charming, it was cost effective, since the bark was salvaged from a lumber mill near the coast.

In 1926 the Redwood Highway opened from Grants Pass to Crescent City, and automobile-fueled tourism was ready to roar. With a wildly popular traveling route, a stunning cave with tours, and plans for a Swiss-inspired village under way, things looked promising. Then the Great Depression hit. But that didn't stop the small-town visionaries and their contractor/architect Gust Lium from continuing plans and building the signature structure at the caves. It was Lium, a local contractor, who selected the unique site for the Chateau and conceived its design. The Chateau's Oregon originality continues inside with a two-sided limestone and marble fireplace, and Douglas fir, madrone, ponderosa pine, and white oak are used throughout the structure. Tucked into the ravine, the Chateau remains as much a part of the lore of the monument as the marble and limestone caves it was named after.

> **Details:** At Cave Junction, Oregon, on U.S. 199, take Oregon 46 to its end, Oregon Caves National Monument. The National Park Service operates all cave and interpretive tours March through November and manages the monument; the Chateau is open May through October. Phone (541) 592-3400 or visit www.oregoncavesoutfitters.com; monument information is found at www.nps.gov/orca/.

WHERE THERE'S A CAVE, THERE MUST be cavemen. In the case of Grants Pass, the closest large town to Oregon Caves National Monument, local business promoters decided that playing off the popularity of the caves was a natural way to promote the region. In 1922 they established the Realm of the Cavemen, a group whose mission was more than primitive haute couture. Dressed in animal skins and wigs and brandishing

bones and clubs, the cavemen (and a cave queen) made public appearances with a specialty of surprising visiting political dignitaries and robbing them of their dignity.

Thomas Dewey, Richard Nixon, John and Jacqueline Kennedy, Robert Kennedy, and Ronald Reagan were all "initiated" into the Realm of the Cavemen, whether they wanted to be our not. Such is life on the campaign trail.

An 18-foot fiberglass reminder of those days stands in front of the Grants Pass Chamber of Commerce and Visitors Center at NE. Sixth Street and Morgan Lane. According to Hank Geiske, one of the "cavemen," the big man was created by the International Fiberglass Company in Venice, California, then hauled by truck to Grants Pass, where it has stood during decades of controversy over its appropriateness.

The curious read the interpretive sign next to the gigantic Neanderthal man, then often step inside to ask more about the caveman: "We do have a lovely historic district, too," implored the volunteer hoping, to steer visitors to more seemly points of Grants Pass.

The Grants Pass Visitors and Convention Bureau created a new marketing icon named The Guide. Graphic artist Michael

Schwab designed the city's new "brand," a woman river rafter meant to "reflect the adventurous and independent spirit, a spirit that typifies many who call the Grants Pass area home." To date, she has yet to be duplicated in fiberglass.

> **Details:** The Caveman and Visitors Center are at NE. Sixth St. near Interstate 5.

Central Oregon

The center of Oregon serves up a region of contradictions. The volcanic past has left the Cascade Range covered with dense forests to the west, the haunting beauty of the high desert pocked by cinder cones and singular rock formations to the east. A region whose weather is defined by sunshine, not rain, bucks the Oregon stereotype held by strangers. Amidst this is what man has created. Contemporary life, natural beauty, and history clash and mesh, each jockeying for a position to settle into the next century.

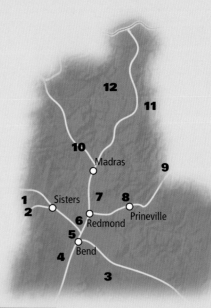

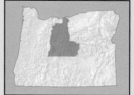

South Sister and Soda Creek

1	Mt. Washington	**7**	Smith Rock State Park
2	Dee Wright Observatory	**8**	Wildland Firefighters Monument
3	Pine Mountain Observatory	**9**	Painted Hills
4	Sunriver Resort	**10**	Museum at Warm Springs
5	Old Mill District	**11**	Big Muddy Ranch
6	Petersen's Rock Gardens	**12**	Sherar's Falls

THE CASCADE RANGE REACHES FROM northern California into British Columbia, Canada. This 20- to 50-mile-wide ribbon of volcanic history both defines and divides Oregon. To the west is the lush Willamette Valley, and on the east the high desert. Thought to be named after the cascading waterfalls on the Columbia, the range is a series of stratovolcanoes (more often called shield) of various evolutions, massive lava flows (often mistaken for severe forest fires by those not in the know), basalt layering, and cinder cones that offer up a compilation of volcanic history.

This isn't your run-of-the-mill old Pliocene-Pleistocene bunch of andesite volcanoes but rather a Pleistocene volcanic platform of overlapping basalt and basaltic andesite lava flows divided into two subprovinces, Western Cascades and High Cascades.

The stretch of range seen in central Oregon from viewpoints on the eastern side is predominately part of the younger 3.5 million-year-old High Cascade. Each peak from Mt. Bachelor to the south to Mt. Hood north can be seen from here: Mt. Bachelor, 9,065 feet, home of the state's premiere ski area; South Sister, 10,358 feet and one of the "Three Sisters," the youngest and tallest of the siblings; Broken Top, 9,175 feet, its southeastern flank dramatically altered by glacier erosion and volcanic forces; Middle Sister, 10,047 feet and one of the region's composite volcanoes; North Sister, 10,085 feet with about a third of its base eaten away by glaciers; Three-Fingered Jack, 7,841 feet of jagged beauty; Mt. Washington, 7,794 feet; Mt. Jefferson, 10,495 feet; and on a clear day, Mt. Hood, 11,239 feet, home of Timberline Lodge (see p. 48).

Looking at this set of peaks may lead to the question: what's that odd-looking point atop Mt. Washington, and is it holding something back? The peaked protrusion on this shield volcano—forming the pinnacle that sets this apart from the other mountains—is a single micronorite plug, or lava plug. Mt. Washington is less than 100,000 years old, big but dormant, so it won't be blowing that plug.

Other Peaks and Their Eruptive Status

Mt. Hood: This 11,239-foot stratovolcano is the highest peak in Oregon and also the most active. During the past 30,000 years lava domes have bulged from it and collapsed, creating huge flows that built a fan on the south and southwest flank. The most climbed peak in the Cascade Range, Mt. Hood erupted in 1853, '54, '59, and '65. Remember its neighbor, Mt. St. Helens?

Mt. Jefferson: The upper cone of this stratovolcano formed only 100,000 years ago. Although there have been two minor debris flows, in 1934 and 1955, Jefferson's fit of volcanic eruptions ended about 50,000 years ago. Still, geologists say it "cannot be regarded as extinct."

Three-Fingered Jack: This shield volcano has more in common with Mt. Washington than is easily visible: inside the glaciated shield is a pyroclastic cone under the summit minus the plug. This is what Mt. Washington might have looked like if the lava plug hadn't formed. Categorized as dormant, erosion will continue to change its face.

South Sister: Modest eruptive and long-term action took place here until about 2,000 years ago. To get the full picture, hikers trek up to the snow-filled caldera of this, Oregon's third-highest peak. The word from volcanologists is that this composite volcano (along with Middle Sister and Broken Top, all composite volcanoes) "may erupt explosively in the future."

Mt. Mazama: Mt. Mazama blew off nearly 4,000 feet of its peak about 7,700 years ago in an epic eruption that spewed ash as far as Canada and left 22 inches of the stuff near what is now Bend. The caldera formed from the eruption is Crater Lake.

Newberry Volcano: This broad shield volcano was created by thousands of eruptions that began about 600,000 years ago. Its proximity to the Cascade Range has little to do with its origin; Newberry's 500-square-mile volcanic sprawl is part of the High Lava Plains. Some of the history is recent (only 1,300 years ago), and it is not over; geologists predict activity in the future. What you see now at its center is a collapsed caldera filled by two lakes (Paulina and East), with the 7,984-foot Paulina Peak jutting to one side. Newberry Volcano National Monument, a treasure of volcanic debris, is 20 miles southeast of Bend off U.S. 97.

Lava Butte: This little 5,000-foot cinder cone is part of the massive Newberry Volcano. The Lava Lands Visitor Center is a good place to start, but a hike to the visitor rest area at the summit gives a spectacular view of the basaltic andesite flow that blankets 5 miles of land to the north and 3 miles to the west until it stops at the Deschutes River. That all happened about 6,100 years ago. Once a cinder cone has erupted, that's it. Lava Butte is south of Bend off U.S. 97.

Pilot Butte: Not every town has a cinder cone within its city limits, but Pilot Butte is one of Bend's best-known landmarks, and it's also a state park. You can drive (certain months of the year) or walk to the 4,138-foot summit for a spectacular sunset or sunrise. The park entrance is off U.S. 20 (Greenwood Ave.) on Bend's east side.

Three-Fingered Jack

Newberry Volcano

SNOWPLOWS CLEAR THE MCKENZIE Highway, Oregon 242, between the towns of Sisters and McKenzie Bridge each June, making way for a snail-paced drive through Willamette National Forest. Just as the lush forest scenery lulls you, there is an abrupt visual dead end. Suddenly trees are replaced with black lava rock, part of the Yapoah Crater flow that left 60 miles of jumbled basalt.

Perched on the summit of McKenzie Pass is the quirky Dee Wright Observatory. If you're thinking traditional "observatory," think again. At an elevation of 5,187 feet, this lava structure looks like a boil on the backside of the lava flow. You won't find any telescopes inside, rather viewing windows that frame several of the Cascade Range peaks and buttes. If you wind your way farther up the recently renovated path, you'll find a bronze "peak finder" to further identify mountains, cinder cones, and lava flows in the surrounding panorama. As you look out at all of this, remember that as little as 1,500 years ago basalt flowed from the nearby cinder cones.

The Depression-era observatory construction project was completed in 1935 by the Civilian Conservation Corps, Camp F-23 (Camp Belknap), Company 927. It was designed by a young landscape architect, William Park. But it is Dee Wright, a 24-year veteran U.S. Forest Service horse packer who died while the observatory was under construction, for whom the observatory was named—perhaps because the structure is as unique as its namesake. Wright was born in 1872 into an Oregon pioneering family and grew up among the Milawa Indians. He suffered his fatal heart attack while rowing across the McKenzie River. His ashes were scattered along the summits of the Cascade Range he packed through for decades.

NASA and Lava Flows

In August 1964, with the space race in full gear, the national media converged on the Bend area, and folks were all aflutter over the attention. The region's volcanic history was coming in handy, for NASA now had the idea that astronauts could test their moon-walking skills on like terrain. That surface was found on the lava flows of central Oregon. A fifteen-man NASA crew found the pumice terrain near Crescent in Klamath County "easy" compared with that on the McKenzie lava fields near the Dee Wright Observatory. The astronauts' final stroll (in full lunar garb) was on the obsidian flow at Newberry Crater. The toughest walk: McKenzie lava field.

Places to Observe the Skies

Pine Mountain Observatory: This traditional dome observatory tops Pine Mountain. Follow U.S. 20 southeast of Bend for 26 miles, then 8 miles south at Millican. You will be in the middle of nowhere. The University of Oregon Physics Department operates Pine Mountain's three Cassegrain reflecting telescopes. The public is welcome during the summer. Visit the web site at pmo-sun.uoregon.edu, or call (541) 382-8331.

Sunriver Nature Center Observatory: This is an educational nonprofit group within Sunriver Resort south of Bend, where ten to twenty telescopes can be in use at one time with staff explaining the sights. Located in Sunriver next to Lake Aspen on River Road, (541) 598-4406, www.sunrivernaturecenter.org.

Haggart Astronomical Observatory: The only public observatory in the Portland area, the Haggart is a program of the John Inskeep Environmental Learning Center of Clackamas Community College. 19600 South Molalla Ave., Oregon City. Call (503) 657-6958 xLOOK (5665), or visit the website at depts.clackamas.edu/haggart.

SUNRIVER RESORT OFF U.S. 97 SOUTH of Bend is the area's largest destination resort. But pull into the center of this 3,300-acre complex with 2,900 homes and 900 plus condominiums, an airstrip, and two golf courses built *after* 1970, and there sits what looks like a historic log lodge. That lodge was once the Officers' Mess and Clubhouse of Camp Abbott, a 5,500-acre military training camp that opened May 15, 1943—and closed a year later.

Now called the Great Hall, the first portion of the Officer's Mess, built of logs and stone, was completed by the end of 1943, and the rustic mountain lodge Clubhouse was built in April 1944 in part as a training exercise. Prior to its dedication, the local newspaper called it an "architectural triumph of engineering trainee skill." Designed by Capt. John V. Banks and built by the Army Corps of Engineers, the two-story hall has a footprint of 50 by 96 feet and the

charm of a historic lodge. Exposed interior hewn timbers and rafters were harvested from the surrounding property and stone was quarried from eastern Oregon. An open interior mezzanine, two circular stairways—one around a 56-inch-wide ponderosa pine—and a massive stone fireplace dominate the room with its open truss gable roof design.

The camp was constructed as a self-contained community that trained 10,000 soldiers in 17-week shifts. In June 1944, Camp Abbott closed and the remaining 2,500 members were relocated to Ft. Lewis, Washington. Within six weeks, all buildings were auctioned off or torn down and salvaged.

The Bend Elks Lodge purchased the Clubhouse, left it in place, and used it for country dances. Most of the camp acreage was sold to a Prineville cattle operation, and at one point the exquisite Clubhouse was used as a barn. It was even the set for a segment of the popular TV western "Have Gun—Will Travel."

The property's current incarnation as Sunriver Resort began in 1965 when John Gray and Donald McCallum bought the land; plans for Sunriver Resort were proposed in 1969. The dilapidated Clubhouse was restored and reopened as the Great Hall.

Where's the Rest of Camp Abbott?

Post Chapel: There were three chapels on the base; only the Post Chapel was salvaged. It was dismantled and moved to Third St. in Prineville, where it served as Our Savior's Lutheran Church.

The Lodge at Summer Lake: Frank and Ruth Graves purchased two former barracks at the Camp Abbott auction and moved the buildings in 8-foot sections to their lodge site in south-central Oregon (photo lower left). The barracks are being used as sleeping rooms, and some have been combined and opened up into a great room. (See Summer Lake, p. 74.)

Pawn Shop: Dozens of houses in Bend were built from the dismantled lumber. The Pawn Shop on Third St. is said to have been (appropriately) built from Abbott's second-hand lumber.

Bureau of Land Management Warehouse: One of the barracks is now used for fire management storage by the Bureau of Land Management in Prineville on Seventh off Harwood going west.

THREE SHIMMERING SILVER SMOKE-stacks with an American flag perched top and center define Bend's "skyline." The stacks were part of the 1915 Power House that churned the production of lumber in what was once a thriving timber town. Nearby is the 1937 barn-red Crane Shed, designed for sorting and storing timber. It's hardly a traditional shed, 500 feet long, 74 feet wide, and 50 feet high with distinctive arched roof and timber exterior buttresses. A massive 70-foot traveling crane mounted on the interior framework moved the timber. The shed had an unusual conversion to tennis courts in the 1960s, and later to a beverage distribution center.

The smokestacks and gutted brick Power House at their base, a few of the Mill A buildings, and the Crane Shed are all that remain of the mills that supported the community. Instead of the smell of rotting wood chips and freshly cut lumber is the scent of a new kind of money. Today, where mills once produced a million board feet of lumber a day and the smokestacks spewed black soot over the town, stands an upscale shopping district with dozens of office and residential buildings along beautifully landscaped roads.

Set along the Deschutes River, a parcel adjacent to what once held freshly cut trees in a "holding pond" is a small public park. The old tuff stone railway station was moved to the Old Mill District from its site along the tracks to make way for a highway, where it now serves as an art center. The mill's shift whistles no longer blow, but during the summer strains of music can be heard from the Old Mill District amphitheatre. Sipping a glass of merlot, listening to Bob Dylan sing along the idyllic Deschutes River, it's hard to imagine the backbreaking millwork that built the town.

Bend's first big timber mills opened in 1916 when Shevlin-Hixon Company began milling the landscape in facilities west side of the river. A month later, the rival Brooks-Scanlon started operating at its Mill A com-

plex east of the river, expanding into Mill B site in 1922. Between them was one of the largest lumber operations in the nation; Brooks-Scanlon owned 145,000 acres of forest when its mill opened, and by 1924 Shevlin-Hixon was cutting 200 million board feet a year.

By 1937, the U.S. Forest Service declared that the mills were overcutting their renewable supply of lumber, and Bend had about 20 years to live. The next year Brooks-Scanlon Mill A closed down, and in 1950 Shevlin-Hixon sold its interest to Brooks-Scanlon. Final owner, Crown Pacific Ltd., closed the remaining mill in 1994.

Bend had a second economic coming

based on tourism and construction and boomed from the 1950 population of 11,409 to 55,000 in 2003. Developers purchased much of the mill property for development of the Old Mill District in 1993. The Power House and smokestacks are the logo for the Old Mill project; the smokestacks were refurbished, but no specific plans are under way for the historic Power House.

The fate of the Crane Shed looks grim. In 1982 it was nominated for the National Register of Historic Places. The state deemed it eligible for listing, but the owners requested that the state not forward the nomination. At the time of publication, the Crane Shed—the only one remaining in the state—stands empty and is in jeopardy of being demolished.

Details: Follow Old Mill District signs west off U.S. 97 (Bend Parkway) to Powerhouse Drive, Bend.

THE HIGH DESERT LANDSCAPE OF central Oregon is broken to the west by the Cascade Range. To the east along U.S. 97 north of Redmond juts a vertical slice of pillars and sheer red cliffs that seem to be perennially bathed by the setting sun. Smith Rock State Park, a 641-acre gem, sits on the edge of the lava plains like the jutting backbone of a stegosaurus. Over millions of years, the Crooked River slowly worked its way through a pile-up of volcanic ash, rhylotic lava, and mud flows, cutting a canyon of pillars and cliffs. Wind and water erosion added to the artistry, creating strange formations like Monkey Face that stand as sentinels against the blue sky.

But it is the little specs that appear on these spires that make the geologic formations all the more transfixing. More than 1,400 climbing routes snake up the cliffs and pillars, making the site an international rock-climbing destination. Normal folks can park along the rim and, with a pair of binoculars, observe climbers as they pick there way up the walls. There are also hiking trails that take you to the starting point of many routes.

> **Details:** East off U.S. 97, 9 miles northeast of Redmond, turn east at Terrebone onto NW. Smith Rock Way and follow the signs.

What Else Rocks in Central Oregon

Petersen's Rock Gardens: Perhaps Smith Rock and Petersen's Rock Gardens are the yin and yang of rockery in central Oregon. One is a natural phenomenon, the other a manmade creation that is folk art at its finest.

In 1906, Denmark native Rasmus Petersen immigrated to central Oregon. He cultivated the dust of the high desert into farmland, but in his backyard he took what the region was best known for—rocks—and in 1935 began building castles with moats full of water lilies, churches with steeples, and villages on miniatures hillsides with water-

falls. Neighbors were entranced, and he continued with a patriotic theme of an American flag, Statue of Liberty (carved from a single boulder), and grounds full of peacocks, grass, picnic tables, and chairs. Most of the rocks came from within an 85-mile radius of the gardens. Obsidian, lava, agate, jasper, petrified wood, and the infamous thunder eggs (Oregon's state rock) are stacked and tucked and laid out in a crazy quilt of ingenuity.

Mr. Peterson died in 1952, but the rock recreations stayed put. Sue (Mr. Petersen's granddaughter) and her husband George live in the 1927 family home and care for the grounds and run the museum. The Rock Gardens may be a quick stop for tourists needing a break from Highway 97, but one should really spend an hour or so. There are no interpretive signs, no identification of the rocks, so you can let your imagination go!

About half of the Gardens' visitors are from out of state. The strangest question of the owners: "Didn't Walt Disney buy this place?" Admission is by donation and the Gardens are open 365 days a year. Follow the signs west off U.S. 97 between Redmond and Bend; it's about 3 miles off the highway.

Steins Pillar: It looks darn phallic, and it takes some walking to see it, but the 400-foot-high volcanic plug protruding from the pine forest is unusual. From Prineville, drive U.S. 26 east for 9 miles to Mill Creek Road, near the end of Prineville Reservoir. Continue on Mill Creek Road for 5 miles, turn onto Road 500, go for about 2.5 miles, and park in the turnoff at the trailhead.

Twin Pillar: This is the smaller version of Stein's Pillar just a couple of miles away.

The Ship and the Island: These formations are just a few of the incredible piles of eroded volcanic debris in Cove Palisades State Park. The park headquarters and campground sit near the base of the Ship, ash-flow tuffs and sediments eroded into the shape of a ship. The Island, opposite the Ship, is sedimentary layers of the Deschutes Formation and part of the Newberry volcanic flow. This is what this area would look like if man had never touched it. Drive 11 miles north of Redmond on U.S. 97 to the Culver/Cove Palisades exit and follow signs about 6 miles.

SINCE 9/11, PUBLIC MONUMENTS TO heroes and heroines who have lost their lives seem, perhaps, small. But they say mountains about people who chose such dangerous occupations, their reasons and goals. This becomes all the more noble

died in the explosive Storm King Mountain fire near Glenwood Springs, Colorado. The loss was devastating, and the grief swallowed the town.

Two years later, that loss and grief transformed into the Wildland Firefighters

story of those lost on Storm King Mountain. The memorial path is lined with gentle aspen and red-twig dogwood; set amidst the greenery are twenty large boulders, symbolizing the twenty-person fire crew. Signage on some of the boulders gives information about hotshot crews (the name is in reference to their being in the hottest part of fires) and firefighting. Then there are the faces: plaques are secured to fourteen of the boulders with the photo, name, and description of each of the firefighters and how they felt about their job, the outdoors, life in general.

The following are the Oregon hotshots lost that day on Storm King Mountain:

Kathi Beck, 24, Eugene
Tammi Bickett, 24, Powell Butte
Scott Blecha, 27, Clatskanie
Levi Brinkley, 22, Burns
Doug Dunbar, 22, Springfield
Terri Hagen, 28, Prineville
Bonnie Holtby, 21, Prineville
Robert Johnson, 26, Redmond
Jon Kelso, 27, Prineville

Details: Prineville is at the junction of Oregon 126 and U.S. 26 northeast of Bend; Ochoco Creek Park, 450 NE. Elm, Prineville.

when friends, family, or a community embrace such a loss so completely as happened in Prineville, a high desert lumber town, the county seat of Crook County and home to the Prineville Interagency Hotshots, a top-notch crew of firefighters.

Since 1980, Prineville has been the home base of the Hotshots and a source of civic pride. That pride turned to horror on July 6, 1994, when nine members of the hotshots were among fourteen firefighters who

Monument, honoring all firefighters, past, present, and future. The Prineville Hotshots Parents Committee spearheaded the effort, along with community volunteers and U.S. Forest Service personnel. Dedicated in 1996, the memorial stands in Ochoco Creek Park near downtown Prineville. The bronze statue of three firefighters, two men and one woman, is symbolic, but it is the 100-foot pathway that meanders along Ochoco Creek that tells the

Bowman Museum, Prineville

This charming museum, housed in the 1910 Crook County Bank building, constructed of locally quarried basalt, features a small exhibit about the Wildland Firefighters. The museum also features exhibits on central Oregon's rich pioneer history. 246 N. Main St., Prineville; call (541) 447-3715 for museum hours.

JOHN DAY FOSSIL BEDS NATIONAL Monument straddles central and eastern Oregon, offering a portfolio of millions of years of geologic history embellished by the effects of tumultuous weather. The 14,000-acre natural exhibit is divided into three units: Clarno, Sheep Rock, and the stunning Painted Hills.

Each unit offers up a gallery of earthly delights, but Painted Hills with its soft bands of undulating, mineral-created colors is the hands-down crowd pleaser. Thousands of tourists find their way to the Painted Hills lookout or follow a half-mile trail through this canvas. It's like finding your self in Oz.

The 3,132-acre Painted Hills unit is not a fly-by-night creation. It took over 33 million years to get things just right. Volcanic ash deposits, changes in ancient soils and vegetation, and a drastic cooling all contributed to a color palette that varies with the light. To see the hills at their best, visit in the late afternoon when the low light plays off the hills. Come April and May, the wildflower season adds another layer to the landscape.

> **Details:** The road to the Painted Hills unit is clearly marked on U.S. 26 between Prineville and Mitchell.

HALF OF THE PEOPLE WHO STOP FOR Mary Hore's marionberry cobbler at Antelope Store and Café ask the same question: "Where was that cult place, that Rajneesh Ranch?" Served up with a deep dish of warm cobbler are directions to what was Big Muddy Ranch, then Rancho Rajneesh, and now the Washington Family Ranch, Wildcat Canyon home of the evangelical Christian teen camp Young Life.

The 64,000-acre hideaway is easier to find now that the county paved the road. "Follow Cloud Camp Road to Muddy Road, about 22 miles; just follow the blacktop," Mary explained for the thousandth time. "Whatever Satan will use for evil," added Don Hore of the destination, "the Lord will use for good."

Those who follow the route through land of volcanic outcroppings, sage, big sky, and stunning vistas finally pull up to the historic ranch house, wander to the bunk house (now a visitor center), and load into a four-wheel-drive vehicle with a couple of volunteers for a tour of the ranch. Three hours later, with stories of more miracles than are found in the New Testament, you get the picture. Big Muddy Ranch, aka Rancho Rajneesh and now home to Young Life, serves up hardcore Christianity to teens in an incredible camplike setting. Clean-cut kids in search of Christian fundamentals live in a lawn-green oasis in dorms around landscaped courtyards, play basketball, skateboard, swim, scream over the lake on zip lines, learn teamwork on rope courses, and eat meals in a dining hall with blaring Christian rock in the background. Everybody is pumped up on Jesus, and not ashamed to say so.

The 88,000-square-foot meeting hall, where only two decades ago guru Bhagwan Shree Rajneesh held court before thousands of red-clad Rajneesh devotees, is now a sports center where Young Lifers can work out on four basketball courts, a rock climb-

ing wall, weights and exercise machines, pool tables, and a skateboard park.

The home of the most notorious cult in Oregon history has a new population of believers with a very different vision. The white-bearded Bhagwan Shree Rajneesh, who turned a one-time cattle operation in the middle of the high desert into the ulti-

mate cult community, would probably be envious. This seems to be working.

The Bhagwan was on the run from the law in Poona, India, home of his ashram, when he came to America in search of a new base. The Rajneesh Foundation International laid down $5.75 million for the 82,000 acres of overgrazed land 22 miles from the town of Antelope, population 40. The historic Big Muddy Ranch was no more;

it was renamed Rancho Rajneesh. The property was still zoned for cattle ranching, but the foundation spent $120 million to ready the land for the devotees. That included construction of a 44-acre reservoir, a 53-car garage for the Rajneesh's Rolls Royce fleet, and a paved 4,500-foot airstrip for easy exits from his new and growing domain.

Rancho Rajneesh was platted with power and water for a town of 20,000. Members

had a disco to boogie at, townhomes, cottages or dorms to live in, a massive meeting hall where they paid homage to the Rajneesh, a shopping mall, offices, workshops, even a hotel, all surrounded by miles of desolate central Oregon landscape and policed by their own armed Peace Force.

Followers had come from all over the world to help create the commune. In their spare time, they took over the tiny burg of

Antelope. When locals questioned their plans, they managed to secure enough votes to take control of the town and rename it Rajneesh. The one café and general store was bought and renamed Zorba-the-Buddha Rajneesh. Led by the Bhagwan's chief aide Ma Anand Sheela, they made life hell for anyone who crossed their path to righteousness. From 1981 to 1985, life for anyone other than a Rajneeshee was ugly.

Not content with running the town of Antelope, cult members set their sights on Wasco County. The Bhagwan bused in and

registered homeless people from across the country so they could cast their ballots for Rajneesh candidates in the 1984 Wasco County election. That plan failed, but it got the attention of state officials.

What was the beginning of the end of the steamroller that was the Rajneesh Foundation was the only documented incident of bioterrorism in the United States. The plan was to sicken a good portion of the population in The Dalles by contaminating the water system on Election Day, thus swaying the votes. To test out their plan, Rajneeshees went to The Dalles and sprinkled salmonella on the town's restaurant salad bars. Ten salad bars were hit, and more than 700 residents became ill. The second election-tampering plan also failed, and back at the Rancho things were rocky. Cult informers were slipping information to authorities on plots from poisoning to murder. Even the Bhagwan verbally attacked Sheela and her allies to the press.

On Oct. 23, 1985, the Bhagwan, Ma Anand Sheela, and six followers were secretly indicted by a federal grand jury for immigration crimes, and then the Wasco County grand jury returned indictments against Sheela and two others, charging them with attempted murder of the Bhagwan's personal doctor. By this time, Sheela was on her way to Germany, and the Bhagwan was nabbed in North Carolina attempting to flee the country.

In the end, Sheela and twenty followers were indicted on federal charges and civil lawsuits. Sheela's counts included attempted murder and poisoning. The Bhagwan paid $400,000 and left the country; he died in 1990 in India at the age of 58. In December 2002, a former Rajneeshee voluntarily returned and pled guilty to attempted murder of then Oregon's U.S. attorney, Charles Turner. Seven people were indicted in the murder conspiracy. One remains at large in Germany.

Rajneeshees left the Rancho in busloads, and the site turned into one of Oregon's largest ghost towns. In 1991, Montana millionaire Dennis Washington bought the property with the intention of developing it into a destination resort. Unable to get land-use variances for the resort, he sat on the property while considering returning it to a cattle ranch. At the same time, Young Life needed a new camp in the region. One

ceeded with the transformation of the Rancho into a camp for Christian teens.

The Washington Family Ranch is one of twenty-five Young Life camps in the United States. Antelope is on Oregon 218 northeast of Madras. A monument at the base of the flagpole by the Antelope post office reads: "Dedicated to those of this community who throughout the invasion and occupation of 1981–1985 remained, resisted and remembered. 'The only thing necessary for triumph of evil is for good men to do nothing.'"—Edmund Burke

Christian conversation led to another, and Dennis Washington and Young Life were hooked up. Washington eventually donated his $3.5 million investment to Young Life for use as a youth camp and gave an additional $2 million to create the sports center.

Back in Antelope, folks were a bit nervous about another religious group so close on the Big Muddy Ranch property. They took a leap of faith, and Young Life pro-

The Rajneesh Go to the City

In addition to the Big Muddy Ranch, during the early 1980s the Rajneesh opened the Rajneesh Hotel on Portland's South Park blocks and Zorba the Buddha disco at SW. 10th Ave. and Pine St. On July 29, 1983, bombs exploded on the second and third floors of the hotel, injuring only the bomber.

Historic Oregon Cults

At one time the Cult Resource Center in Portland listed 200 "cults" in the state. Dozens of cults recruit and function in Oregon, but the following along with Bhagwan Shree Rajneesh and his followers are perhaps the most famous.

Church of the Bride of Christ: In 1902, Joshua the Second (aka Edmund Creffield) founded the "church" and rounded up a devoted flock of "holy rollers." By the time he got to Corvallis, the townfolk were not happy, and Creffield was tarred and feathered before he was sent to the slammer for adultery. That was just the beginning of Creffield's woes. When he was released from the penitentiary in 1906, he was shot and killed by the brother of one of Creffield's teenage conquests. The young man was found innocent of murder under an insanity plea (one of the first in the state), but his sister shot and killed him after the trial. Not the end. The young girl and Creffield's legal wife both committed suicide. Oh, yes, Edmund Creffield and many of his flock lived in Walport.

Heaven's Gate: The folks who gave San Diego, California, the 1997 mass suicide of thirty-nine experienced their first revelation and began cult recruitment at a campground near Gold Beach on Oregon's southern coast in 1975. Leader Marshall Applewhite, along with Bonnie Lu Nettles, took the names Bo and Peep. After the Gold Beach get-together, members attempted other recruitment meetings including one in Walport, where they promised salvation by spaceship. About thirty in the audience became believers long enough to skip town. The group morphed into various incarnations until they resurfaced as Heaven's Gate with the idea that they would die and be transported on a spaceship trailing the comet Hale-Bopp. The mass suicide coincided with the comet's 1997 appearance.

THE HISTORY OF INDIAN RESERVATIONS in the United States is not a pretty story. But it is only part of the legacy of the Warm Springs Tribe and its 640,000-acre Warm Springs Reservation. That story is told within the walls of the Museum at Warm Springs. The 25,000-square-foot award-winning design replicates a traditional encampment set along Shitike Creek amidst the cool branches of towering cottonwoods. The varied roof lines and textural materials incorporate native designs and symbols: longhouse, tepee, drum, dance bustle, flowing creek, and patterns of a huckleberry basket are woven into the architecture. Donald J. Stastny designed the museum, the first tribal museum in Oregon. The museum was 20 years in the planning, and in 1988 a tribal referendum was voted on to appropriate $2.5 million for the museum construction. The completed project cost $7.6 million.

"By 1955, we realized that we were going to lose our history," explained Chief Delvis Heath. "We put $50,000 aside to purchase artifacts. Then we had some money, and began the museum. We finally got the museum built for the people. If you really want to learn about your past, who you are, you can come to the museum."

Visitors enter under the TWANAT sign, meaning "to follow (traditions and culture)," into a tower with a circle that represents the circle of life. From there they are caught up in an evolving story of beauty, bravery, and brutality. The permanent collection of artifacts—many saved from financially strapped tribal members selling their family heirlooms to collectors—historic photographs, murals, and documents chronicle the tribal history. The sadness of these exhibits is countered by beautiful recreations of a Wasco wedding, a Paiute family wickiup, a Warm Springs tepee, and a cedar plank house. A series of oral histories by the elders are both informative and heartwarming. The museum is intended, not only to educate non-Indians, but to save the "old ways" for Native American generations to come.

> **Details:** 2189 U.S. Highway 26, north of Madras. Open seven days a week, 362 days a year from 9 A.M. to 5 P.M., (541) 553-3331, www.warmsprings.com.

Brick and Mortar Reminders of the Past

North of the Museum at Warm Springs along U.S. 26 within the Warm Springs community stand reminders of the past. The Bureau of Indian Affairs built reservation boarding schools across the country. The first school in Warm Springs appeared in 1862, but permanent dormitories, classrooms, and a commissary were built in 1897. These boarding schools were set up to assimilate Indians into white culture. Native clothing, long hair, language, traditions, and religion were forbidden. Children were deloused, hair shorn, and clothes replaced. Parents were off limits, and white teachers and matrons took over. The system, while disastrous to the indigenous culture, remained until 1961 when the schools were taken into the local school district. The dormitories closed in 1967, and three of the red brick school buildings remain and are used by the tribe for a Community Counseling Center and Education and Cultural Heritage Department. The old boarding school next to the tennis courts is not in use. The red brick buildings can been seen on the west side of the highway within the Warm Springs community.

THE SCAFFOLDS LOOK PRECARIOUS, the poles and nets cumbersome, the crashing water of Sherar's Falls treacherous, and the fishermen undaunted. Just north of Maupin on the Deschutes River is one of the remaining places where loop nets outnumber fly rods—where the traditional fishing grounds of the Pacific Northwest Indians have not been flooded, leaving behind broken treaties, bitterness, and memories.

When Terry Courtney Jr. begins to explain the choreography of net fishing, it's like hearing Jerome Robins wax eloquent about a ballet. "Everything moves in a circle," he explained as he waited in his home on the Warm Springs Reservation for the fall steelhead run. Mr. Courtney was ready. His scaffold and platform were constructed on the Deschutes, 10- to 18-foot nets woven, Douglas fir poles dried, peeled, and trimmed, smokehouse readied, and pick-up truck just waiting. Before Mr. Courtney began dip net fishing he was, "you know, just a fly fisherman." His devotion to traditional fishing is legendary. In addition to fishing, he serves on the Columbia River Inter-Tribal Fish Commission.

While the wooden scaffolds that jut off the basalt rocks of Sherar's Falls look rickety, Mr. Courtney explains that the platforms, their locations handed down through families, sit securely on two reinforced legs set onto a rock with stringers and cross stabilizers to keep the platform from moving forward and back. The whole thing is counterbalanced in the back with rocks. To build one, you must learn how from the tribal elders. Elmer "Scotty" Scott taught Mr. Courtney. The scaffold and platforms are removed every year and rebuilt in the spring.

There are two different net fishing techniques: dip and set net. Dip net fishermen plunge the nets into the edge of the river, whereas the set nets are just that, set in place off the edge of the platform. The nets billow out 4–9 feet. Neither technique is for the impatient. "There's lots of waiting," Mr. Courtney said, but when the salmon or steelhead surge upstream, the fishermen are there.

> **Details:** Warm Springs Reservation fishing below Sherar's Falls is clearly marked for tribal members only, but visitors can watch from the campground or road on either side of the Deschutes off U.S. 216 near Sherar's Bridge north of Maupin.

Books

Barlow, Jeffrey G., *China Doctor of John Day*. Binford & Mort, 1979.

Battaile, Connie Hopkins, *The Oregon Book of Information A to Z*. Saddle Mountain Press, 1998.

Fisher, Jim, *Gilchrist: The First Fifty Years*. Oregon Color Press, 1988.

Friedman, Ralph, *Oregon for the Curious*. Caxton Printers, rev. 1993.

Jordan, Tom, *Pre: The Story of America's Greatest Running Legend, Steve Prefontaine*. Roadside Press, 2d ed., 1997.

King, Bart, *An Architectural Guide to Portland*. Gibbs Smith, 2001.

Nesbit, Sharon, and Tim Hills, *A History of the Multnomah County Poor Farm*, McMenamins, 2002.

Peters, Shirley, and Sheila Smith, *Hot Lake, the Town Under One Roof*. self-published, 1997

Palahniuk, Chuck, *Fugitives and Refugees: A Walk in Portland, Oregon*. Crown Publishers, 2003.

Randall, Warren R., *Manual of Oregon Trees and Shrubs*. Oregon State University Press, reprint ed., 1981.

Walth, Brent, *Fire at Eden's Gate*, Oregon Historical Society Press, 1994.

Wortman, Sharon Wood, *The Portland Bridge Book*, Oregon Historical Society Press, 2001.

Wright, Thomas L., and Thomas C. Pierson, *Living with Volcanos: The U.S. Geological Survey's Volcano Hazards Program*, USGS Circular 1073.

Periodicals, Studies, and Documents

Big Muddy Ranch, Oregon Sheriff–Wasco County website.

Boardman, S. H., Letter to Mr. C. H. Armstrong, November 1951, Silver Falls State Park files.

Bulleit, William M., Classic Wood Structures, *Pacific Builders and Engineer*, October 1943, and May 1948.

Deschutes Historical Center, Architectural Plans, Camp Abbott [Maps], 1943–1945.

Environment & Climate News, July 2001.

Ex-cultist Admits Guilt, Faces Jail in Murder Plot, Associated Press, *Seattle Times*, December 22, 2002.

Grossman, Lawrence K., The Story of a Truly Contaminated Election, *Columbia Journalism Review*, January/February 2001.

The History of NAS Tillamook and Its Role in World War II, Tillamook Air Museum.

Klamath Basin Drought Series, *Bend Bulletin*, May 14, 2000.

Klamath Project Operations Draft Environmental Impact Statement (DEIS) Scoping document, May 2003.

Learning From Portland, *Architecture*, March 1991.

National Registry of Historic Places Inventory Nomination Forms, Oregon State Historic Preservation Office, Salem.

New Carissa Wreck, Timeline of Events, *Oregon Live (Oregonian)*, 2003.

The Nine States of Oregon series, *Oregonian*, Nov. 11, 2003.

Oregon Public Library Online History Project, Oregon State Hospital, Oregon Blue Book (online), and the official websites of the agencies listed above.

The Rajneesh Ranch Reborn, by Steve Duin, *Oregonian*, September 5, 1999.

Recent Paleolimnology of Upper Klamath Lake, Oregon, JC Headwater, Inc., Roseburg, Oregon, March 16, 2001.

Restoration of the Historic Columbia River Highway, Hood River to Mosier Section 2000, Oregon Department of Transportation.

Relation between Selected Water-Quality Constituents and Lake Stage in Upper Klamath and Agency lakes, Oregon, USGS Water-Resources Investigations Report 96-4079 summary.

State of Oregon Inventory of Historic Properties, Brooks Scanlon Crane Shed, *Bend Bulletin* April 25, 1944; April 30, 1960; July 12, 1961.

Two Rajneeshee Members Plead Guilty, by Mark Larabee, *Oregonian*, December 16, 2000.

Various studies, Oregon Emergency Management, Department of Geology and Mineral Industries, and National Tsunami Hazard Mitigation Program.

Interviews

Jim Adler, Eric Bergland, Mark Darienzo, Gil Ernst, Bob Favret, Robert Frasca, Tim Hills, Steve Janiszewski, Faye Kesey, Judy Koonce, Steve Lent, Sam Naito, Shirley Peters, Matt Rabe, Jim Renner, Bill Russell, Ben and Connie Smith, and many others whose interviews added to the pleasure of researching this book.

Christine Barnes is the author of the award-winning *Great Lodges of the West, Great Lodges of the National Parks, Great Lodges of the Canadian Rockies, El Tovar at Grand Canyon National Park,* and *Old Faithful Inn at Yellowstone National Park. Great Lodges of the West* was the inspiration for a four-part PBS television series that first aired in 2002; *Great Lodges of the Canadian Rockies* will air as a two-part PBS series in 2004. Christine served as senior consultant on both projects. Her first book, after an 18-year career in newspaper journalism, was *Central Oregon, View from the Middle,* so it was a natural to branch out into every part of Oregon for this book. Christine and her husband, Jerry, who shot the majority of the book's photographs, spent four months touring Oregon, staying predominately in state parks where they found shelter in a covered wagon, yurts, tepees, and cabins. They usually live in a house in Bend, Oregon.